R. L. P. AND
DOROTHY M. JOWITT

Discovering
Walks in
Wessex Towns

SHIRE PUBLICATIONS LTD.

Photographs are acknowledged as follows: Gordon J. Scriven, plate 1; Cadbury Lamb, plates 2, 8, 9, 10, 11; Jeffery W. Whitelaw, plates 3, 18; Jane Miller, plate 4; Mrs E. Preston, plate 5; E. V. Tanner, plate 6; Robert E. Jowitt, plate 7; Mr Peberdy, Curator of Southampton Museums (copyright Southampton Corporation), plate 12; David Uttley, plates 13, 15, 17, 20, 21; John Haddon, plate 14; Robert D. Bristow, plate 16; G. H. Haines, plate 19; G. N. Wright, plate 22.

On the maps of the towns car parks are denoted by the letter P, and public conveniences by the letter C. Arrows denote the direction of traffic in one-way streets.

Contents

Blandford Forum

History. In spite of its name, Blandford Forum is not a Roman town. It had a market as long ago as 1215, and sent two members to Parliament in 1305. Blandford, like other old towns, suffered severely from fires, and the fifth and last, on 4th June 1731, consumed almost the entire town. Starting in a tallow-chandler's shop (where the King's Arms inn is now) the fire, fanned by a strong north wind, was soon completely out of control. It was blown right across the town, and loose pieces of burning thatch were even blown across the river Stour, spreading the fire to the village of Blandford St Mary. So hot was the conflagration, that three fire-engines were burnt out, the church and four hundred houses were destroyed, and thirteen lives lost. Money for relief poured in, headed by £1,000 from George II.

As London had Sir Christopher Wren to rebuild the City in 1666, so Blandford had the brothers John and William Bastard, local architects, to rebuild both the church and the town in the dignified style of the eighteenth century.

Approach. Enter from Salisbury by A354. After passing the bus station on the left, turn left at the Badger Hotel (on the right), into Damory Street. At the far end of this, turn right into East Street, pass the church and Market Place on the right, drive down West Street and the car park is on the left. (From Bournemouth, A350, cross the bridge and the car park is on the right.)

Walk. Turn left out of the car park on to the **bridge**, which displays a notice threatening transportation for life to those who damage the bridge. There is pretty river scenery and a good view of the old town and church. Return past the car park and follow West Street back to the town. On the left is the very successful modern Georgian **Crown** hotel (1) (Magnus Austin, architect). As the street bends right into the Market Place, there is an excellent view of the **Town Hall** (2) and church (plate 2), only the twentieth-century Midland Bank being out of proportion to the neighbouring buildings. On the right, facing up Salisbury Street, is the former Greyhound inn (3), now the **National Westminster Bank**, with highly ornamented front. Further along is the **Red Lion** inn (4), with a huge red lion in the pediment. On the churchyard corner is the **Fire Monument**, in the form of a little Doric temple, commemorating 'God's dreadful visitation by fire'.

The **church** (5), SS Peter and Paul, stands magnificently in the centre of the town and is a copy-book example of a city church.

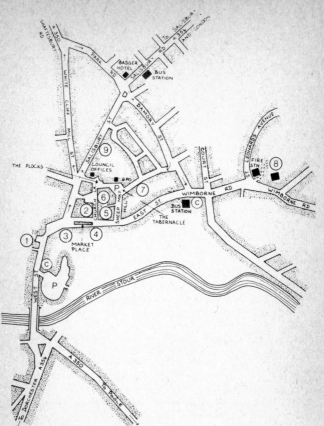

BLANDFORD FORUM

1. Crown hotel
2. Town Hall
3. National Westminster Bank
4. Red Lion
5. Church of SS Peter and Paul
6. Legion House
7. Old House
8. St Leonard's Chapel
9. Ryves Almshouses

The Bastard brothers had originally intended to add a spire to the tower; a cupola was erected instead, but not by the Bastards. The interior is most imposing, especially the tall Ionic columns of Portland stone. Note the west gallery with fluted Ionic columns, the organ, from the Chapel Royal of the Savoy in London, and the elegant font. The chancel, dating from 1893, occupies the old site of the apse, which the architect, Robert Norman, daringly moved on rollers to its present site.

Turn up Church Lane. On the right is **Legion House** (6), generally considered the finest house built in Blandford since the fire. It has a good staircase with rococo ceiling above it and panelled rooms. Turn right into The Plocks, and on into **The Tabernacle**, a triangular open space where a temporary church was built after the fire. Beyond this is a street named The Close. On the right is the **Old House** (c. 1660) (7) which survived the fire. It was built by a German doctor named Sagittary. It has remarkable ornamentation carved out of the solid brickwork and two magnificent chimney-stacks.

Turn down Damory Street, and left into Wimborne Road, to see **St Leonard's Chapel** (8), a medieval leper hospital now used as a barn, along a footpath by the fire station on the corner of St Leonard's Avenue. Return along The Plocks to Salisbury Street and turn right. A little way up, on the right, are the **Ryves Almshouses** (1682) (9), which also escaped the fire. Notice the fine panelled chimney-stacks. Return to the car park straight down Salisbury Street and West Street.

In the neighbourhood. Three miles north-west along the Shaftesbury Road (A350), beyond Stourpaine, is **Hod Hill,** a magnificent Iron Age camp with a Roman fort in the north-west corner. Close by, on the north, is **Hambledon Hill**, another very fine Iron Age camp.

Bournemouth

History. Bournemouth, now one of England's foremost seaside resorts, was almost non-existent until Squire Tregonwell of Cranborne built himself a marine villa in 1810. The **Exeter Hotel** (1) in Exeter Road incorporates a portion of this villa, which is commemorated by a plaque.

From Bournemouth's sandy cliffs there are magnificent views to the Isle of Wight in the east and to Swanage in the west. There are beautiful sands, charming gardens and parks, and every sort of amusement.

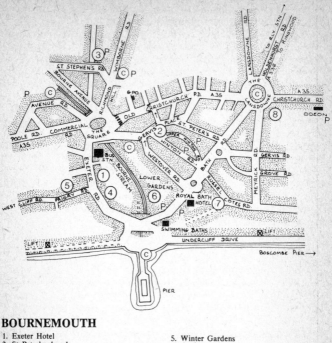

BOURNEMOUTH

1. Exeter Hotel
2. St Peter's church
3. St Stephen's church
4. Punshon Memorial Church

5. Winter Gardens
6. Pavilion
7. Russell-Cotes Art Gallery
8. Municipal College

Approach. Approaching from the east by Christchurch Road (A35), take the second turn left out of the Lansdowne Round-about, Bath Road, and there is a car park on the left at the bottom of the hill. (There are several other car parks, including a multi-storey one in Hinton Road. If all the central ones are full, the visitor can usually find space in one behind the Odeon cinema just before the Lansdowne Roundabout and can take a bus from there to the town centre.)

Buildings of most architectural interest are **St Peter's church** (2) at the corner of St Peter's Road and Hinton Road, by Street, architect of the London Law Courts, and **St Stephen's church** (3), in St Stephen's Road, by Pearson, architect of Truro Cathedral. The **Punshon Memorial Church**, in Exeter Road (4), is a remarkable modern building. The **Winter Gardens** (5), home of the famous Bournemouth Symphony Orchestra, and the **Pavilion** (6) in Westover Road are the largest places of entertainment. The **Russell-Cotes Art Gallery** (7) is in an old villa in Russell-Cotes Road, East Cliff. At the Lansdowne is the **Municipal College** (8) at the back of which is the public library, housing a very interesting collection of photographs of old Bournemouth.

West of the Pier, Priory Road leads from Exeter Road into West Cliff Road, from which there are left turns into West Overcliff Drive and the **Chines**, very pretty steep wooded ravines leading down to the sea.

Skerryvore, a house in Alum Chine Road (west of West Cliff Road), where Robert Louis Stevenson once lived and wrote some of his books, was destroyed by bombs, and has now been made into a memorial garden.

Note. Many new roads are being made, and one-way streets frequently altering, so the map cannot be guaranteed beyond the time of going to press.

Bridport

History. 'Stabbed with a Bridport dagger' was a local expression for 'hanged' — Bridport has been famed for its ropes for many centuries. In the seventeenth century, when the government established other rope-walks, the trade fell, but with the rise of the Newfoundland fishing industry Bridport soon regained its prosperity by net-making. It became, and remains, the largest centre of net manufacture in Europe. One Samuel Gundry set up his net-works in 1665, and his name remains in the present firm of Bridport-Gundry Ltd.

The town's first charter was granted by Henry III in 1253. From Edward I's reign until 1868, Bridport returned two members to Parliament. A thrilling incident occurred in 1651, during Charles II's escape after his defeat at Worcester. Failing to obtain a ship for France at Charmouth, Charles and his party rode boldly into Bridport and had a meal at the George inn. The yard was full of Parliamentary soldiers. Charles, disguised as a manservant, pushed past them clumsily and was cursed for his rudeness. On leaving the inn, he decided to seek safety in the remote country north of Bridport, so he and his party turned left into a by-lane

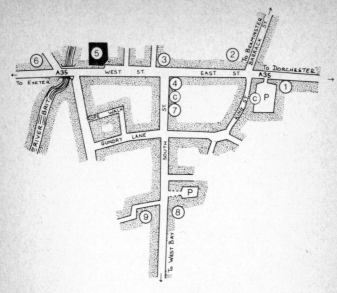

BRIDPORT

1. No 74 East Street
2. Unitarian Chapel
3. Beach & Co, chemist
4. Town Hall
5. Rope and net factory

6. St Swithun's, Allington
7. Museum
8. Friends' Meeting House
9. St Mary's church

just outside the town off the Dorchester road (now marked by a monument on the corner of Lee Lane). Their pursuers from Charmouth, thinking that the king had taken the Dorchester road, rode past the by-lane at full speed, and Charles made good his escape.

In the nineteenth century there was shipbuilding at West Bay, the seaside part of Bridport, and now timber is imported there. It is a popular resort of fishermen and yachtsmen.

Approach. The A35 London-Exeter road passes right through the town. Coming from Dorchester, notice Lee Lane with the monument on the right just before Bridport. Enter by East Street. The car park is on the left adjoining the Lord Nelson inn.

Walk. The streets of Bridport are wide and lined with dignified Georgian buildings. **No. 74 East Street** (1) is a very handsome

9

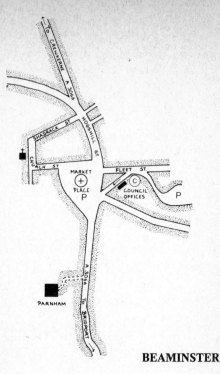

BEAMINSTER

Georgian mansion (c. 1760) on the left. The **Unitarian Chapel** (1794) (2), lying back from the street on the north side, is in the Classical style with Ionic columns supporting the porch; the interior has galleries round three sides supported by Ionic columns. The charming Georgian chemist's shop, **Beach & Co.** (3), is on the site of the former George inn, visited by Charles II. The **Town Hall** (1785-6) (4) stands well at the junction of the three main streets. The council chamber contains interesting mural paintings showing Bridport's old industries. On the north side of West Street is the large **rope and net factory** (5). Just beyond the bridge is a right fork, and shortly on the left the very handsome Georgian (1826-7) **St Swithun's church**, Allington (6). Return to the Town Hall and right into South Street. On the left is the **museum** (7), sixteenth-century, with projecting porch. It is open throughout the year 10.30 a.m. to 1.00 p.m., and from June to October except on Thursdays and Saturdays, from 2.30 to 4.30 p.m. Included in it are the last of the original type of net-making looms (working on Wednesdays and Saturdays in summer), the Omand collection of dolls in national costumes, and interesting Victoriana. The **Friends' Meeting House** (8), also on the left, dates from 1697; connected with it are some almshouses. **St Mary's parish church** (9), opposite, is a large Perpendicular building with Early English transepts. **West Bay** is a mile or two further down this road.

In the neighbourhood. About five miles north of Bridport (leave by Barrack Street) is **Beaminster**, a very charming little town with brown stone houses. The church, St Mary's, has an extremely fine tower, probably very early sixteenth-century, buttressed and richly carved, and some interesting monuments inside.

Christchurch

History. Christchurch, lying between the rivers Avon and Stour near where they join in Christchurch Harbour, is known to have existed in A.D. 900, when it was named Twyneham. The minster, called Christchurch, became very important and finally gave its name to the town. It was a Saxon foundation, and was refounded in 1150 as a priory of Augustinian canons. At the Dissolution the monks' buildings were demolished, but the minster was left as the parish church. The town is now noted for fishing and sailing.

Approach from Lyndhurst by Bridge Street and Castle Street, crossing the fine six-arched bridge over the Avon, and turn left into Church Street. (From Bournemouth approach by Barrack Road and High Street and straight on into Church Street.) Turn right into Church Lane, and left into Quay Road, at the end of which is the car park. (If this is full, there is another on the right at the north end of High Street, where the bypass comes in.)

Walk. From the car park, walk back a few yards to the **Priory** on the right (1) (plate 3). This has a magnificent Norman nave and, outside, a richly decorated Norman circular turret at the east angle of the north transept. The porch is thirteenth-century, and the tower and chancel good fifteenth-century Perpendicular. The rood-screen is fourteenth-century, partly restored, and has some quaintly carved figures. There are carved miserere seats, and many interesting monuments, including the beautiful Salisbury chantry, prepared by Margaret Pole, Countess of Salisbury, for

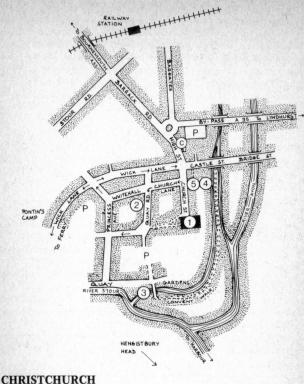

CHRISTCHURCH

1. Priory
2. Red House museum
3. Old mill

4. Constable's House
5. Castle

her own memorial, but never used, as she was beheaded by order of Henry VIII in 1541. The Shelley memorial, under the tower, was refused by Westminster Abbey because of his doubtful religious views and was given to Christchurch by his son. The Lady Chapel at the east end is of earlier work than the choir.

Also in Quay Road is the early eighteenth-century **Red House**, now a very interesting museum (2).

Return to the car park. At the far end of it a path leads out on to the Quay. On the left are public gardens, and ahead is a bridge, to the right of which is an old **mill** (3). Cross the bridge and turn left into **Convent Walk**, a charming footpath between the mill-stream and the Avon. This leads out into Castle Street, and on the left, just short of the street, are the extremely interesting **Constable's House** (4), a most valuable example of Norman domestic architecture with beautiful windows and a fine chimney, and the remains of the **Castle** (5), built by Baldwin de Redvers, a Norman baron, in Henry I's reign. The keep stands on an artificial mound and is approached by a path from Castle Street. From the **King's Head** hotel, a pleasant Georgian building opposite the castle, there is an excellent view of the whole group of priory, castle and Constable's House. Return to the car park by Castle Street and Church Street, passing some pretty old houses, and across the priory churchyard.

In the neighbourhood. Hengistbury Head, between Christchurch Harbour and the sea, can be approached on foot by Wick Lane, ferry across the Stour (summer only) and a field path, or by car via Barrack Road, Stour Road and Boundary Road, the second turn to the left after crossing Tuckton Bridge. It is a promontory fort, and was inhabited from prehistoric times until the fourth century A.D. Bronze Age burial sites, remains of wattle and daub hut villages, British and Roman coins, and many other very early relics have been found there. The double dykes were erected to defend it by land in the Iron Age. The name is a corruption of 'Hednesbury' or 'Hynesbury' and has no connection with Hengist. There are lovely views inland, seaward to the Isle of Wight and the Needles and westward across Poole Bay to Purbeck.

Dorchester

History. Dorchester, the *Durnovaria* of the Romans and the 'Casterbridge' of Thomas Hardy's Wessex novels, is the county town of Dorset. In about A.D. 70 the population of the great entrenched camp of Maiden Castle (see below) was transferred to the site of the present town, where a city, the cantonal capital of the Durotriges, was laid out in the Roman manner, surrounded by a wall. Except for one small fragment the wall has gone, but its lines were marked out in the eighteenth century by the planting of avenues of trees, known locally as 'The Walks'.

During the Saxon period Athelstan, grandson of Alfred the Great, established a mint here. The town probably suffered from Danish incursions. In medieval times King John hunted in the neighbourhood, but nothing remains of the castle in which he stayed, and the county prison now stands on the site. In the seventeenth century the Rev. John White, rector of St Peter's, organised the settlement of New Dorchester in Massachusetts and obtained a charter from Charles I. Seeing the colonists off from Plymouth, White made them promise to build a church on arrival, which they did. The tercentenary of the charter was celebrated in 1930, when the mayor and councillors paid a visit to the daughter town in America.

When the Civil War broke out, John White persuaded the townspeople to declare for Parliament, but the Royalist forces, under Prince Rupert, captured the town with hardly a shot fired. Prince Rupert's men broke into John White's house and stole his books. In 1644, however, Parliamentary forces recaptured the town. In 1685, after the Duke of Monmouth's ill-starred attempt to seize the crown from James II had ended in defeat at Sedgemoor, his wretched followers were rounded up and tried before the infamous Judge Jeffreys. 320 of them were hanged, seventy-four in Dorchester; hundreds more were transported for life to Barbados as slaves.

The most eminent figure of the nineteenth century in Dorset was undoubtedly Thomas Hardy (1840-1928). He was born at Upper Bockhampton, two miles east of Dorchester, where his birthplace is preserved by the National Trust (open March to October, 11 a.m. to 5 p.m.). His heart is buried in Stinsford church, nearby, and his ashes in Westminster Abbey. By his thinly disguised place-names in his Wessex novels, he created the 'Hardy Country' and made Dorset's name famous all over the world.

He is commemorated in Dorchester by the statue by Eric Kennington at the top of The Grove, and also by his room, transferred from his home at Max Gate to the museum, with many other relics such as the manuscripts of his novels.

Approach Dorchester by the A35 from Bournemouth and Poole. (Just before reaching the town, note on the left, in the suburb of Fordington, **St George's church** with a prominent tower. It contains a most interesting Norman tympanum, showing the battle of Antioch, c. 1098, when a vision of St George helped the Crusaders.) The Frome is crossed by two bridges. Affixed to the first is a cast iron notice threatening 'transportation for life' to those damaging the bridge — a relic of early nineteenth-century justice.

Proceed up the High Street to the roundabout (site of the Roman west gate) at the crossroads known as Top o' Town. Take Bridport Road and enter the car park on the right almost immediately.

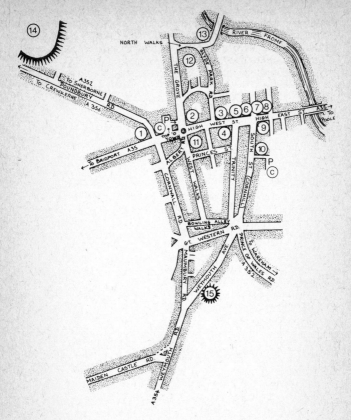

DORCHESTER

1. Dorset Military Museum
2. Hardy's statue
3. Shire Hall
4. Judge Jeffreys' Lodging
5. County Museum
6. St Peter's church
7. Town Hall
8. King's Arms
9. All Saints' church
10. Napper's Mite
11. Roman wall
12. Roman villa
13. Hangman's Cottage
14. Poundbury Camp
15. Maumbury Ring

Walk 1. A short distance along Bridport Road is the **Dorset Military Museum** (1), a tall Victorian gateway now known as The Keep, but formerly the entrance to the Dorset Regiment barracks. It now houses a most interesting collection of military records, and is open Mondays to Fridays 9 a.m. to 5 p.m.; Saturdays 9 a.m. to 12 noon (October to June), 9 a.m. to 5 p.m. (July to September).

Return to the roundabout and, after seeing **Hardy's statue** (2), proceed down High West Street. This is chiefly Georgian in character, having been built after the town had suffered three disastrous fires between 1613 and 1735. There are many old shop fronts and bow windows. A short distance down on the left is the **Shire Hall** (3), which enshrines the old Court Room (enter by No. 58) where the Tolpuddle Martyrs were tried for forming a trade union and asking for a rise of wages from nine shillings to ten shillings per week. They were sentenced to seven years transportation, but were given a free pardon after two years, in 1836. Further down, on the opposite side of the street, is the early seventeenth-century **Judge Jeffreys' Lodging** (4), where he stayed during the Bloody Assize; it is now a restaurant. Beyond this, on the left, is the **County Museum** (1881-3), a remarkable Victorian building with a glass roof supported by cast-iron columns (5). It is open from 10 a.m. to 1 p.m. and 2 p.m. to 5 p.m. and contains, besides Hardy's study, a wonderful collection of prehistoric and Roman antiquities and a very interesting geological section. Just by the museum is the parish church, **St Peter's** (6), a large and imposing Perpendicular building with a rich Norman door. Of great interest are two late fourteenth-century effigies of knights, both reclining on their sides. There is a tablet to the memory of John White and, outside the church, a statue of William Barnes, the Dorset dialect poet (1800-86).

Just beyond the church is the **Town Hall** (7), an effective Victorian building with a clock-tower, and beyond that the comfortable-looking, bow-windowed **King's Arms** hotel (8). Opposite is the former **All Saints' church** (9), with a fine spire, rebuilt 1843-5 on the site of a former church. Threatened in 1970 with demolition, it was fortunately reprieved and will be an extension of the museum. Here turn back, and left into South Street, also known as Cornhill. In the middle of the street is the **Town Pump** (1784). There are some pleasant Georgian buildings, notably the bow-windowed **Antelope** hotel. Further down, on the left, is the curiously named **Napper's Mite** (10), a charming building, formerly an almshouse founded by Sir John Napier for ten poor men in 1610, but now a shopping arcade. At the end of the street, several roads meet at The Junction. From here, turn west along

16

Bowling Alley Walks and right into West Walks, and return to the roundabout, passing the fragment of **Roman wall** (11) on the right just after Princes Street.

Walk 2. From Hardy's statue, walk a few yards down The Grove, and turn right into Colliton Park, where between the county hall and the North Walks, are the fascinating remains of a **Roman villa** (12), including a tesselated pavement. Some finds from this villa are in the museum. North-east of the villa, beyond the North Walks, and near the river Frome, is **Hangman's Cottage** (13), a pretty thatched building thought to have been the home of the man who hanged those sentenced by Judge Jeffreys. Return to High West Street by Glyde Park Road, and turn right to the car park.

In the neighbourhood. **Poundbury Camp** (14), north-west of the town, dates from the Iron Age. It was nearly bisected by the railway, but an appeal to Brunel persuaded him to make a tunnel underneath it instead. To reach it by car, turn right by the Military Museum into Poundbury Road.

From the roundabout, follow Albert Road, Cornwall Road and Maumbury Road. **Maumbury Ring** (15) is on the left where Maumbury Road joins Weymouth Avenue. Of Neolithic origin, it was altered by the Romans and adapted as an amphitheatre. During the seventeenth and eighteenth centuries it was used for public executions, when thousands of people would line its banks.

Cross the railway at lights into Weymouth Road, and shortly turn right into Maiden Castle Road. **Maiden Castle** (about two miles from the town centre) is the finest earthwork in Britain and probably in Europe. It lies on an east to west running ridge and has two humps. The eastern hump was first inhabited during the Neolithic period (c. 2000 B.C.). During the Bronze Age (c. 1800-300 B.C.) there was probably no permanent settlement, but in 300 B.C., during the early Iron Age, a small town arose on the eastern hump, fortified by a single bank and ditch enclosing about sixteen acres. In about 200 B.C. the fortifications were much extended to include the west hump. In c. 100 B.C. the great reconstruction took place, causing the 120-acre castle to assume the form it takes today. Excavations by Sir Mortimer Wheeler during the 1930s added greatly to the knowledge of the site. A discovery of supreme interest was a late Iron Age hoard of 22,260 sling stones from the Chesil Beach. At the time of the Roman conquest, the castle was captured by Vespasian, a general who later became Emperor. Until his reign (A.D. 69-79), but not later, the disarmed inhabitants continued to reside in the castle. In due course they were transferred to the new town on the present site of Dorchester.

Late in the Roman period, a Romano-Celtic temple was built in the deserted castle: by the evidence of coins it would be not earlier than A.D. 375.

Cerne Abbas, eight miles along A352, is a very pretty village with a good church and remains of an abbey. The Cerne Giant, a huge carving, 180 feet high, on the chalk downs, is a relic of a fertility cult, perhaps Romano-British or earlier: it may possibly represent Hercules.

Lyme Regis

History. Lyme is mentioned in the Domesday survey as having four farms and twenty fishermen. Its first charter was granted by Edward I in 1284 and 'Regis' was added to the name after that date. The Cobb, the strong stone pier, dates from about that time, and several later monarchs contributed to its upkeep and improvement. The town was an important port and centre of foreign trade in medieval times. It provided four ships for the siege of Calais and five to fight against the Spanish Armada in 1588. In the Civil War the King's forces, led by Prince Maurice, besieged the town, which was defended for about two months by Blake, later the famous admiral. The Duke of Monmouth landed at Lyme Regis for his abortive rebellion against his uncle, James II. Some of the people supported him, but others were half-hearted, so that the town was not officially involved in the rebellion.

In the seventeenth and eighteenth centuries, as bigger ships were built, Lyme Regis harbour could not take them, so the place declined as a port, but soon found compensation by becoming a very popular watering-place. Among famous visitors were Pitt and Jane Austen. All Jane Austen's admirers look first for the spot on the Cobb where Louisa Musgrove, in *Persuasion,* had her famous fall, which seems to them almost historical.

Approach from Charmouth by A35. Drive through Church Street, Bridge Street, Broad Street, fork left into Pound Street, turn left down Cobb Road (steep hill) and park by the Cobb.

Walk. Walk along **the Cobb**: half-way along is an arm going eastwards into the harbour, and on this is an interesting **aquarium** (1). Return to the front and walk eastwards along the traffic-free Marine Parade. The site of **Jane Austen's house** is on the left (2), but unfortunately nothing of it remains. At the far end, turn left into Bridge Street and right across the bridge over the river Lym. The **Town Hall and museum** are on the right (3). The museum (open 10.30 a.m. to 12.30 p.m., and 2.15 p.m. to 5.30 p.m.) has

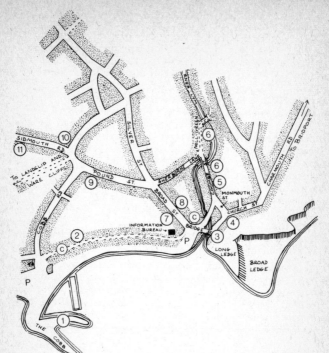

LYME REGIS

1. Aquarium
2. Site of Jane Austen's house
3. Town Hall and Museum
4. Church of St Michael the Archangel
5. Congregational church
6. Mills
7. Three Cups hotel
8. Royal Lion hotel
9. Belmont
10. Coram Tower
11. Umbrella Cottage

exhibits relating to the town's history and a remarkable collection of fossils, for which the district is noted. On the right, in Church Street, is the **parish church of St Michael the Archangel** (4). A Norman church, c. 1100-50, probably built on the site of an earlier one, has been incorporated in the present, mainly early sixteenth-century, building. The Norman nave forms the present porch and part of the tower is Norman. The church contains, among other treasures, a fine carved Jacobean pulpit given by a merchant adventurer in 1613, various memorials to important citizens including a window in memory of Mary Anning (1799-1847), the girl geologist who discovered an ichthyosaurus fossil in 1811, a chained Bible, a copy of Erasmus's paraphrase of St Luke's Gospel, and a Flemish tapestry of a royal marriage, possibly that of Henry VII and Elizabeth of York. Opposite the church is Monmouth Street, which leads into Coombe Street. On the right of this is the handsome **Congregational Church** (1750-5) (5) and beyond this, on the right of Coombe Street and Mill Green, are some interesting old **mills** (6).

Return down Coombe Street to Bridge Street and right into Broad Street. This has some good Georgian houses, including the **Three Cups** hotel on the left (7) and the **Royal Lion** hotel on the right (8). On the left in Pound Street, towards the top, is an eighteenth-century house, **Belmont** (9), with facade marvellously decorated in Coade stone, for Mrs Eleanor Coade in 1784. On the right, where Pound Street leads into Sidmouth Road, is Coram Court, built about 1887 as a theological college, and **Coram Tower** (10), a tower house with pyramid roof (1903-4). Further along Sidmouth Road, on the left, is the fascinating **Umbrella Cottage** (11) with thatched, umbrella-shaped roof.

Note. Lyme Regis is very hilly and a poor walker might be better advised, after visiting the Cobb to drive back again up Cobb Road, and along to Umbrella Cottage, and then turn back, down Pound Street and Broad Street and into a little car park off Bridge Street, and walk to the museum and churches from there.

Poole

History. The old town and port of Poole is situated on a peninsula jutting out into Poole Harbour. It received its first charter in 1248 and has prospered ever since. Always ready to help in defending the country from the French and Spaniards, the town provided four ships and ninety-four men for the siege of Calais in Edward III's time. Harry Page, a fifteenth-century hero of Poole, known to the French as 'Arripay', was a buccaneer who harried both French and Spanish ships, on one occasion taking 120 prizes. The French and Spaniards finally fitted out a joint expedition against him, landed at Poole, plundered the town and defeated Page and his followers, who fled inland.

During the Civil War Poole supported Parliament and was used as a base for the siege of Corfe Castle. Charles II, on his return to the throne after the Commonwealth, had the defences of Poole dismantled, but the townspeople bore no malice and gave him a

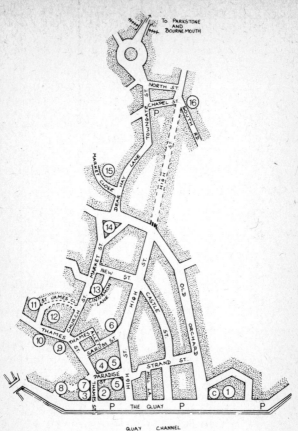

POOLE

1. Poole Pottery
2. Custom House
3. Harbour Office
4. Town Cellar or Woolhouse
5. Warehouses
6. Old Town House or Scaplen's Court
7. King Charles inn
8. Postern Gate
9. Manor House
10. Poole House
11. House in St James' Close
12. Church
13. St George's Almshouses
14. Guildhall
15. Sir Peter Thompson's House
16. Beech Hurst

royal welcome when he visited the town five years later to avoid the Plague in London. During the seventeenth and eighteenth centuries there was much trade with Newfoundland and some handsome houses built by prosperous merchants still remain.

Smuggling was carried on continually, the harbour with its creeks and the heathy country inland being particularly suitable for the contraband trade. In 1747 the 'Free Traders' actually attacked the Custom House and seized and carried away a very valuable cargo of tea which was stored there. The town is now noted for more lawful occupations: shipbuilding and marine engineering, timber, pottery, and light industries of all sorts.

Approach Poole from Bournemouth by A35 and after passing the Poole Civic Centre turn left into A350, Parkstone Road. Follow clearly marked signs to Poole Old Town and Quay, and approach the Quay down Old Orchard. Car parking is allowed along the Quay, and at other places according to where there are demolitions and new developments. The Quay is lined with picturesque old houses and some cosy-looking old inns. The view across the harbour to Brownsea Island with the Purbeck Hills beyond is very fine.

Walk. Start at the east end of the Quay by the famous **Poole Pottery**, founded in 1873 by Jesse Carter (1) (showroom open daily 9 a.m. to 5 p.m.; guided tours of pottery, Monday to Friday by arrangement). Walk westward along the Quay to the **Custom House** (2). This part of the town is a conservation area. The Custom House (c. 1788) is a very handsome building with a pair of curved flights of steps. In front of it is the Town Beam or weighing machine, renewed in 1947. Across Thames Street is the **Harbour Office** (1822), a pleasant building with a colonnade (3). Behind the Custom House is Paradise Street, in which is the **Town Cellar** or **Woolhouse**, a fifteenth-century warehouse (4). Further along, on both sides of Paradise Street, are tall old **warehouses** (5). Turn left from Paradise Street into High Street. On the corner of High Street and Sarum Street is the **Old Town House** or **Scaplen's Court** (6), a prosperous merchant's house of c. 1500. The front part is ruinous, but the remainder is in good order, and is now a museum. In it is a notable Bronze Age dug-out canoe, thirty-three feet in length and one of the longest craft of this date to be found in England.

Return to Thames Street. On the west side of it is the old, timber-framed **King Charles** inn (7). Alongside No. 5 Thames Street is a narrow passage leading to the only piece of town wall still surviving in Poole, and here is a **Postern Gate** (8). Further up Thames Street are two very handsome Georgian mansions, **Manor**

House (9) and **Poole House** (10) and north of the church in **St James' Close** is another fine house (11). All these are outstanding and date from the first half of the eighteenth century.

The **church** (12) dates from 1820 and is a typical example of the Georgian period. The pillars supporting the galleries are of pitch pine from Newfoundland. Church Street and Market Street, into which it leads, both contain many good Georgian houses. On the corner of Church Street and Cinnamon Lane are the picturesque **St George's Almshouses** (13), founded in 1549 but since rebuilt. At the end of Market Street is the very handsome **Guildhall** (14), with curved flights of steps similar to those of the Custom House. It dates from 1761 and is now a museum. Beyond it is Dear Hay Lane, and on the left of this is Market Close, in which is **Sir Peter Thompson's House** (1746), said to be the finest in Poole, and designed by John Bastard, the architect who rebuilt Blandford after the great fire there. It is now Poole Technical College (15). Another very fine house is **Beech Hurst** (1798), now offices, on the corner of High Street and South Road (16).

In the neighbourhood. Poole, whose population of 107,000 made it the largest town in the pre-1974 county of Dorset, includes **Parkstone** and **Branksome**, the sandy beaches of **Sandbanks** and **Branksome Chine**, and the beautiful gardens of **Compton Acres**. Poole Harbour, extending inland towards Wareham, is dotted with islands, the most important being **Brownsea Island**, which the National Trust maintains as a nature reserve. It is thickly wooded and has a lake in the middle. **Brownsea Castle** (1547) was one of a series of forts built by Henry VIII. In 1907 General Baden-Powell held a camp for about twenty boys on this island, and so started the Boy Scout movement.

Shaftesbury

History. Shaftesbury stands about seven hundred feet up on a sandstone spur. King Alfred founded an abbey there in A.D. 880, probably as a place easily defensible against the Danes. His daughter Aethelgiva was the first abbess. In 979 the remains of Edward the Martyr, murdered at Corfe Castle, were brought to Shaftesbury from Wareham and became an object of pilgrimage. King Canute died at the abbey, though he was buried at Winchester. Royal mints issued silver pennies from the abbey until 1272. The abbey and town prospered in Norman times. In the thirteenth century the town became more independent of the abbey and was granted charters for markets. It has remained a prosperous market town ever since, excepting during the Civil War and Napoleonic Wars. The abbey was unfortunately almost entirely destroyed at the Dissolution in 1539.

Approach. Enter by A30 from Salisbury. From Salisbury Street turn left into High Street, and at The Commons turn right into Bell Street. The car park is on the left.

Walk. Turn back to The Commons. The **Grosvenor Hotel** (1) is a pleasant old coaching inn and has, in the upstairs lounge, a remarkable carved sideboard of the Battle of Chevy Chase. From the hotel door, turn left, left again into Bimport and left again into Abbey Walk, from which there is a glorious view over Dorset, Somerset and Wiltshire. Turn left again up Park Walk, and on the left are the **abbey ruins** (2) (open Easter to September, daily

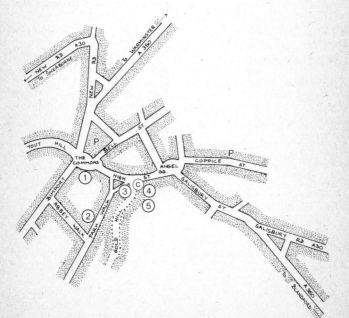

SHAFTESBURY

1. Grosvenor Hotel
2. Abbey ruins
3. Walls of abbey precincts
4. St Peter's church
5. Museum

except Mondays, 10 a.m. to 12 noon and 2 p.m. to 6 p.m.). The townspeople removed most of the stones after the Dissolution, so that little remains of what must have been one of England's most glorious abbeys. The crypt of the Chapel of Edward the Martyr remains, and there is a museum of other relics. A cross, standing on the site of the high altar, was the market cross of St John, moved to the abbey site from Angel Square.

Return to High Street, and turn right into **Gold Hill** (plate 4). This very picturesque, steep cobbled street has old cottages on the left and on the right part of the magnificent buttressed **walls of the abbey precincts** (3). **St Peter's church** (4) by the corner of Gold Hill and High Street, is largely Perpendicular, with a few later additions and alterations. Behind it is the **museum** (5) (open weekdays 11 a.m. to 5 p.m., Sundays 2 p.m. to 5 p.m.), containing items connected with the town's history, and interesting 'bygones' such as a fire engine of 1744, fans, dolls and Valentines.

Sherborne

History. Sherborne's history begins at least as early as A.D. 705, when St Aldhelm became bishop of a new diocese which had been taken out of Winchester. Here at Sherborne he built a cathedral church, to which was attached a body of secular canons. The diocese continued to exist until 1075, when it was transferred to Old Sarum, later Salisbury. During this time the town grew up round the cathedral, which was rebuilt in the tenth century. A doorway showing typical Saxon masonry still exists, in the present Abbey Church (formerly the cathedral). In 998 the Benedictine rule was established and lasted until the Dissolution of the Monasteries by Henry VIII in 1539. The Abbey Church had been rebuilt in the Norman style in the twelfth century. The monks worshipped in the choir of the church, and the townspeople in the nave. During a quarrel in the fourteenth century the townspeople built themselves a new church, All Hallows, adjoining the west end of the Abbey Church. Unfortunately the quarrel grew worse, until a priest of All Hallows, according to an old account, 'shot a shaft with fier' into the thatched roof of the Abbey Church, causing such a conflagration that the whole church was defaced, and the bells and leaden part of the roof melted. This happened at a time when the Norman choir was being rebuilt in the Perpendicular style by Abbots Brunyng and Bradford but the work was eventually completed by the rebuilding of the nave, also in the Perpendicular style, by Abbot Ramsam, and the glorious fan-tracery roof was completed from end to end. In 1539, after the Dissolution, Sir

John Horsey, chief steward of the monastery, acquired the Abbey Church. The townspeople then decided to buy it from him, for about £320, and pulled down most of All Hallows church. Some of the abbey buildings were purchased by the School (founded by a royal charter of Edward VI in 1550).

Industries in the town have included agriculture, gloving, soft drinks and silk, the last dating from 1740, even earlier than the Macclesfield silk industry. The old silk-mill is now incorporated in the modern Marglas fibre-glass factory in the south-west of the town. Sherborne is also a centre of education.

Just outside the town to the east, a castle was built by Bishop Roger (1107-39), Chancellor to Henry I. Sir Walter Raleigh built a large mansion, now known as Sherborne Castle, on the other side of the river Yeo. This was later purchased by the Digbys, the chief family of Sherborne.

Approach by the A30 (from Shaftesbury). Before reaching the town, and shortly after crossing the railway, fork left down Oborne Road; there is a good view of the Old Castle on the left. Oborne Road leads on into Long Street and a turning on the left of this leads into Culverhayes car park.

Walk 1. Turn left out of the car park into Long Street. At the end of this is the sixteenth-century, Perpendicular-style **Conduit** (1), formerly situated in the cloister court of the abbey. Pass this and go through the Cemetery Gate to the **Abbey Church** (2). On the way, on the left, is the **museum**. Notice on the east bay of the church the royal arms of Edward VI, between twisted 'barley-sugar' columns. On the left is a Gothic monument to G. D. Wingfield Digby (1884) who benefited the town in many ways. The south porch of the Abbey Church is partly original Norman, but the upper storey is a Victorian restoration. At the west end are some remains of All Hallows church, the east end of which joined on to the west end of the Abbey Church. In the west porch is a tablet, commemorating the fact that the Abbey Church escaped unharmed in a heavy air-raid on Sherborne in 1940. Enter by the west door, from which there is a magnificent view of the fan-tracery roof. Note the huge columns in the nave, with Perpendicular panelling. At the west end of the north aisle is the Saxon door (see above). The north transept is twelfth-century work; to the east of it is the Wykeham Chapel, in which is the rich canopied tomb, with recumbent effigies, of Sir John Horsey (1564) and his son. The choir contains ten canopied stalls, largely modern, but incorporating quaintly carved fifteenth-century arm-rests. The reredos dates from 1858.

Return to the north choir aisle, where there are two Purbeck-

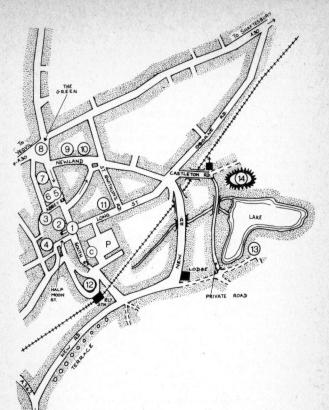

SHERBORNE

1. Conduit
2. Abbey Church
3. Sherborne School
4. Almshouse
5. Abbeylands
6. Abbey House
7. Abbey Grange
8. The Green
9. Lord Digby's School
10. Manor House
11. Red House
12. Pageant Gardens
13. Sherborne Castle
14. Old Castle

marble tombs, one of Abbot Clement (c. 1160), and the other, much mutilated, of a prior in mass vestments. At the east end of this aisle are two stone coffins, formerly thought to be those of King Alfred's brothers, Ethelbald and Ethelbert (860), but now believed to be thirteenth-century.

The ambulatory opens into the Lady Chapel by a beautiful Early English arch. This chapel was of three bays, but at the Reformation two were destroyed and the third converted into a residence for the headmasters of the School. They used it for over three hundred years, but in 1921 the surviving bay of the Lady Chapel was reincorporated into the church, some domestic-looking windows and a fireplace being relics of its former use. Eastward of the original bay, a sanctuary was added on the site of one of the destroyed bays, by W. D. Caroe, architect. In the south choir aisle is the recumbent effigy, in Purbeck marble, of Abbot Laurence (1246-60). The south transept, which is Norman, contains an elaborate monument to John Digby, third Earl of Bristol (1698), with his first and second wives, the signed work of John Nost, a famous Flemish sculptor. The window, showing ninety-six figures carrying the Latin text of the *Te Deum*, was designed by Pugin, the famous nineteenth-century ecclesiologist. St Catherine's Chapel, westward, contains the tomb of John Leweston and his wife (1584).

The conventual buildings of the abbey lay to the north of the church and what remained after the Dissolution is now part of the buildings of **Sherborne School** (3). Adjoining the north-west corner of the nave of the church is the monks' 'Guesten Hall' (fifteenth-century), now the School library. Below this is the Muniment Room, in which a Saxon wall with 'long and short' work has come to light. Here is kept the School's foundation charter of Edward VI (1550). North of this is the School chapel, formerly the abbot's hall, fifteenth-century on a Norman undercroft. East of this, the abbey kitchen, with its huge chimney, still survives.

South-west of the Abbey Church is the **Almshouse of St John the Baptist and St John the Evangelist** (4) dating from 1437 (open 2 p.m. to 3.45 p.m., and 4.45 p.m. to 6 p.m.). The original licence to found it, granted by Henry VI to Robert Neville, Bishop of Salisbury, is still preserved. The management of the almshouse has always been in the hands of twenty brethren, who annually elect one to be Master. The beneficiaries are twelve poor men and four poor women. The south range of buildings (1439-44) is a perfect example of a monastic infirmary; the chapel is open internally to the dormitory, which is two-storeyed, the men sleeping below and the women above. A new wing, added in 1858 by William Slater, architect, blends harmoniously with the older buildings. The chapel contains a very fine late fifteenth-century triptych: in the centre is the raising of Lazarus. The south window contains glass from c. 1475, showing the Blessed Virgin with the two St Johns.

From the almshouse proceed eastward along Half Moon Street, in which is a charming Tudor terrace, c. 1532-4, built as a row of shops with a church room above. This street leads back to the Conduit.

Walk 2. From the Conduit, walk up Cheap Street (Saxon for Market Street), the main shopping street. In and near it are many picturesque houses and shops. These include **Abbeylands** (5), sixteenth-century half-timbered and gabled; **Abbey House** (6), Georgian, in Abbey Road; **Abbey Grange**, formerly part of the tithe barn (7), in Hospital Lane, and, in **The Green** (8), the Dorset County Library and George Inn, sixteenth-century, and Greenhill House, fine seventeenth-century. At the top of Cheap Street turn left into Newland. Sherborne's finest mansion, **Lord Digby's School** (for girls) (c. 1720) is on the left (9). Beyond it is the **Manor House**, now council offices, partly Perpendicular and partly early nineteenth-century 'Gothick' (10). Turn right down St Swithun's Road, and right into Long Street. This also has charming houses, including **Red House** (c. 1730), of red brick with stone dressings (11). Return to the car park on the left.

The castles. Drive out by South Street. On the right are the **Pageant Gardens** (12), commemorating a pageant at the Old Castle in 1905. Cross the railway and turn left into New Road. A footpath climbs up to The Terrace, from which there is a very fine view of the town and abbey. Turn round and drive along New Road to the **Castle** (13). A gateway by the Victorian architect, Philip Hardwicke, leads into the drive. Sir Walter Raleigh, having tried unsuccessfully to restore the Old Castle, built this one in 1594. After Raleigh's fall from favour under James I, Sir John Digby bought the house in 1617, and added four wings to make it H-shaped in honour of Henry, Prince of Wales. The Digby family still owns the house. In the eighteenth century 'Capability' Brown, the famous landscape gardener, dammed the river Yeo and formed a lake, across which is a beautiful view of the Old Castle. The 'new' castle is open to the public from Easter until the end of September, 2 p.m. to 6 p.m., on Thursdays, Saturdays and bank holidays (guided tours). It contains many beautiful rooms full of treasures. North-west of it is the **Gothick Dairy**. A most colourful Roman pavement, found in the park, has been relaid here; it depicts Apollo with a lyre and Marsyas with a double flute. **Raleigh's Seat**, at the north end of the Pleasure Gardens, is the traditional site of his smoking and being dowsed with water by a servant, who thought he was on fire.

Return to New Road and turn right at the Lodge. Just after the crossroads, turn right into Castleton Road. Castleton is a picturesque hamlet with a seventeenth-century late Gothic church. By it is the gateway leading to the **Old Castle** (14). It is a typical fortified dwelling of the twelfth century. The principal remains are those of the keep, the curtain wall and the gateway. There are also some remains of Raleigh's attempted additions and alterations. During the Civil War the Old Castle, held by the Royalists, was twice besieged and much damaged, and was afterwards allowed to go to ruin. The Old Castle is open at the following times: November-February, weekdays 9.30 a.m. to 4 p.m., Sundays 2 p.m. to 4 p.m.; March, weekdays, 9.30 a.m. to 5.30 p.m., Sundays 2.30 p.m. to 5.30 p.m.; April, weekdays and Sundays, 9.30 a.m. to 5.30 p.m.; May-September, weekdays and Sundays, 9.30 a.m. to 7 p.m.; October, weekdays 9.30 a.m. to 5.30 p.m., Sundays 2 p.m. to 5.30 p.m.

Sturminster Newton

History. Sturminster Newton, a charming old market town on the river Stour, was inhabited from Roman times, and probably earlier. The 'minster' part of the name comes from an association with Glastonbury Abbey, and Hinton St Mary Manor, nearby, was associated with the abbesses of Shaftesbury. At Hinton, too, was found the wonderful fourth-century Roman mosaic (now in the British Museum), believed to include a portrait of the head of Christ.

Approach by A357 from Blandford. On the left, just before turning right into Sturminster, are the few overgrown fragments known as the **Castle** (1), actually the remains of a fourteenth-century manor-house. Around the mound are a bank and ditch, suggesting that it was an Iron Age promontory fort it is strictly private.

Drive into Sturminster across the beautiful medieval stone **bridge** (2), with six pointed arches, over the Stour (plate 5). This is another bridge, like those at Dorchester and Blandford, with a notice threatening transportation for life to those damaging the bridge. Turn right up Church Lane; the car park is near the church.

Walk. St Mary's church (3) was originally Perpendicular, and the tower, aisle walls, aisle arcades and nave waggon-roof remain,

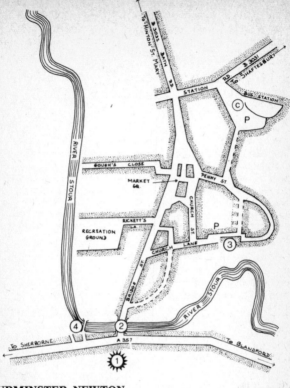

STURMINSTER NEWTON

1. The 'Castle'
2. Bridge
3. St Mary's church
4. Newton Mill

but the rest was largely rebuilt in 1825-7. There is a lectern in memory of William Barnes, the Dorset poet, born in the parish. Walk along Church Street to the **Market Square**: in both are some charming old houses. From the Market Square walk down Gough's Close to the Stour: a pretty path southward along the river bank leads to **Newton Mill** (4), which was working until 1971. Cross the river by a footbridge; a footpath and lane lead to the 'Newton' part of Sturminster Newton, with some pretty old thatched cottages. Return to the town by the main bridge; a field path to the right, just after bridge, leads back into Church Lane.

In the neighbourhood. Fiddleford, about one mile east has a fourteenth-century manor-house, being restored by the Department of the Environment. The Mill House nearby has an inscription (1566) in verse, welcoming visitors and urging the miller to be honest.

Swanage

History. Swanage, until the early nineteenth century a stone-built village with its back to the sea, was the port of export for Purbeck marble, sent all over the kingdom. Sixty quarries were working in 1821. Princess (later Queen) Victoria visited Swanage before her accession in 1837. Later two Swanage men, John Mowlem of the firm of Mowlem & Co., and his nephew George Burt, became contractors in London, and Burt became a sheriff. They collected a vast number of relics of old London and sent them to Swanage; they also began the building boom of the 1880s, which made Swanage a popular watering-place.

Approach from Wareham by A351, and enter Swanage by High Street and shortly fork left into Victoria Avenue. About three-quarters of a mile along this there is a car park on the right.

Walk 1 (through the town). Go on down Victoria Avenue to the sea front and turn right. The **Mowlem Theatre** (1), a fine, modern place of entertainment, dates from 1966. Outside it is a column with cannonballs on top. Curiously, this commemorates King Alfred's victory over the Danish fleet, which took place about five hundred years before the invention of gunpowder! Proceed along Institute Road, the principal shopping centre, and turn right into High Street. On the right is the **Town Hall** (2) in which George Burt incorporated the former front of the Mercers' Hall, Cheapside. It is mid-seventeenth-century and richly carved. Nearly opposite is **Burt's house** (1875) (3), a flamboyant Victorian building, now a convent. Turn down a passage to the left of the Town Hall, and behind it is the old town **lock-up** (1803) (4). **St Mary's church**, King's Road (5), has a plain fourteenth-century tower, but is otherwise Victorian. Nearby is the old mill pond, surrounded by typical stone-built Purbeck cottages. Return to the car park past the cemetery and by Northbrook Road.

Walk 2 (about two miles each way). As in Walk 1, go along Institute Road to High Street, and left along this to the pier entrance. Beyond this is a path on the left, adjoining the entrance to

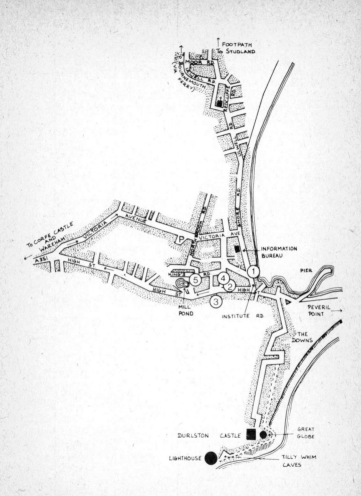

SWANAGE

1. Mowlem Theatre
2. Town Hall
3. George Burt's house
4. Town lock-up
5. St Mary's church

the Grosvenor Hotel. This leads to Peveril Point, past Burt's Gothick **clock-tower**, formerly on London Bridge as a monument to the Duke of Wellington, but now without its clock! Now walk along the cliff path past an open space on the right called **The Downs**. The footpath, well signposted, then goes inland for a short distance and leads into Belle Vue Road. About half a mile further on is **Durlston Castle**, described cynically as 'a stronghold of the bank holiday period', but actually a restaurant. About fifty yards down the cliff is the **Great Globe**, weighing forty tons, dating from 1887. All this area was laid out by George Burt from 1862 onwards. The path continues along the cliff top to **Tilly Whim Caves** and **Anvil Point lighthouse**. (Buses run back to Swanage during summer season.)

Walk 3: to Studland (about three miles each way, or bus no. 7 from Information Bureau).

From Victoria Avenue, turn left along the front, and up Ulwell Road to All Saints church. Go on up Redcliffe Road, left into Moor Road and almost at once right. Pass Hill Road on the left and then follow a footpath, passing Whitecliff Farm on the right. This path leads across Ballard Down to **Studland** (about two and a half miles), a very pretty well-wooded village with a good sandy beach. The church is a very fine example of a wholly Norman church. An alternative footpath leads along the cliff top to Standfast Point and the **Old Harry Rocks** (about four miles).

Wareham

History. Wareham was a Saxon town, though laid out in the Roman manner. It was defended on the north, east and west by earthen ramparts and on the south by the river Frome. Originally the ramparts were crowned with a stone wall, but nothing remains of it. The ramparts have been dated to the ninth century and the grid street-plan to the late Saxon period. There was constant strife between Saxons and Danes; on one occasion the Danes burnt the whole town. During the troubles of Stephen's reign he besieged and finally captured the town, burnt it and occupied the castle. In the Middle Ages the town prospered and became a notable port, being on a tidal river. During the Civil War it changed hands several times. In 1762 it had another severe fire, on a Sunday when most people were in church. 133 houses were destroyed. After this no more thatched houses were allowed. Those still standing, in North Street, probably mark the limit of the fire in this direction.

Approach. Coming from Bournemouth and Poole, enter the town

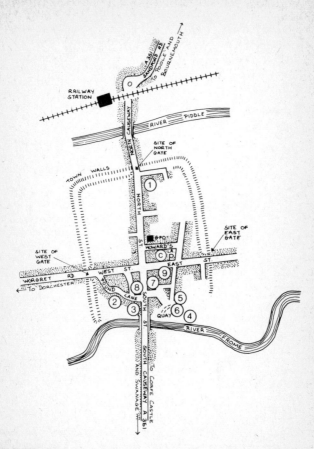

WAREHAM

1. St Martin's church
2. Site of castle
3. Holy Trinity church
4. Granary
5. Church of Lady St Mary
6. House on site of Priory
7. Manor House
8. Black Bear inn
9. Streche Almshouses

past the railway station, which bears the coat of arms of the former London and South Western Railway (1840-1923), along the North Causeway, across the river Piddle and past the site of the North Gate by the Saxon church, on the left. Drive along North Street, and by the GPO turn left into Howard's Lane, where there is a car park.

Walk. From Howard's Lane, turn right and shortly left into East Street. Turn left, and in about 200 yards is the town wall and site of the East Gate. Walk northwards along the wall and turn left at the north-east corner. This leads to the site of the North Gate, and **St Martin's church** (1). This is the most perfect Saxon church in Dorset, typically high and narrow, with 'long-and-short' work at the angles. It dates from 1030-1100. About 1200 a north aisle was added. The little tower dates from the sixteenth century. In the church there are traces of much wall painting and the recumbent effigy, by Eric Kennington, of Lawrence of Arabia, who lived near Wool for the last years of his life.

Cross the road and ascend Shatter's Hill and resume the walk along the walls: this stretch is most impressive. Near the north-west corner is a spot known as **Bloody Bank**, where some of Monmouth's followers are said to have been hanged after the defeat at Sedgemoor (1685). At the site of the West Gate, turn left into Pound Lane. The site of Wareham's vanished **castle** (2) is on the right. Excavations revealed foundations of a Norman keep dating from the twelfth century. From Pound Lane walk along to the very picturesque Quay, beside the river Frome. **Holy Trinity church** (3) (fourteenth to sixteenth centuries), on the right of South Street, long disused, has been restored for use as a parish hall. On the Quay is a fine old eighteenth-century **granary** (4), now a cafe, and lovely views over the marshes to the Purbeck Hills. The **church of the Lady St Mary** (5) (plate 6), believed to be the only one with this dedication, is reached through a passage. The Saxon nave was destroyed at a disastrous rebuilding in 1841; there is a picture of it in the church. It was the original church of the monastery of St Aldhelm, founded in 700. The Perpendicular tower survives, and the chancel with some good Decorated windows. On the south side of the chancel are two chapels, one Norman and the other Decorated. Other items of interest are the leaden font, a great rarity, with twelve figures round it — presumably the twelve apostles, two Purbeck-marble effigies of knights, the coffin in which the murdered King Edward the Martyr was laid until his remains were removed to Shaftesbury Abbey and an inscription to Hutchins, the county historian (1773). Of outstanding interest are some Saxon inscriptions dating from the seventh to the ninth centuries. South of the church is a sixteenth-century house, standing on the site of a twelfth-century priory (6).

Resume your walk up South Street. On the right is the **Manor House** (7) with stone front (1712), and opposite the bow-windowed **Black Bear** inn (8), with a fine model black bear on the balcony. At the crossroads turn right into East Street. On the right are the **Streche Almshouses** (9) (1741). From here return to Howard's Lane.

In the neighbourhood: Corfe Castle (5 miles). Leave Wareham by South Causeway (A351). Corfe Castle was important even in Saxon times, but its most prosperous period was the thirteenth century, when the Purbeck marble quarries were sending marble to churches all over the country.

The magnificent **castle** with its great Norman keep, towering over the village, stands on a conical hill in a gap in the downs, and must have been impregnable before the invention of gunpowder. For two centuries a royal castle, it was used as a state prison: Edward II was taken there after his deposition. Lady Bankes's spirited defence of the castle during the Civil War, while her husband was away with the King, is famous. When the castle finally fell by treachery, it was blown up, but the gunpowder only dislodged the towers, tilting them at crazy angles.

The **church** is dedicated to King Edward the Martyr, young king of the West Saxons, murdered by his step-mother Elfrida so that she might put her own son Ethelred the Unready on the throne. The tower is Perpendicular; the body of the church was beautifully rebuilt in Victorian times (1860). An excellent model of the village and castle, when perfect, is near the Square.

Weymouth

History. Weymouth and Melcombe Regis, two ancient boroughs divided by a harbour, formerly each sent two members to Parliament. They were connected only by a ferry worked by a rope, but in 1571 the two boroughs were amalgamated and a bridge was built. In 1780 the Duke of Gloucester, brother of George III, visited Melcombe Regis for his health and built himself a house, now the Gloucester Hotel. On his recommendation, the king went there in 1789, to the joy of the townspeople. His first bathe is amusingly described in Fanny Burney's diary. The court and many fashionable people followed his example, hoping to be cured of gout and rheumatism. The cramped little town spread northward, numerous handsome terraces being built on the curve of the bay. The old town across the harbour was not affected by the development but, oddly enough, its name of Weymouth, instead of that of Melcombe Regis, is now generally used, though the shops, pier, beach and railway station are all in the latter.

Approach from Wareham by A353. Note on the right, after passing Osmington and the Plough inn, a fine view of the downs, with a **white horse** ridden by George III cut in the chalk in 1815, the only one of many such white horses to have a rider. Next comes **Preston**, with old village and church and vast modern developments. Then pass the low-lying tract of Lodmoor on the right, and enter Weymouth. Drive along the front to the Jubilee Clock (Victoria, 1887) and turn right into King Street; the car park is on the left opposite the railway station. (Other car parks are in Gloucester Mews and St Nicholas Street.)

Walk 1. Start from the **Jubilee Clock** (1) and proceed northward (left). On the left is **Royal Crescent**, planned as a crescent but built as a terrace. Beyond this is **Belvidere**, another Georgian terrace, and beyond that the stately, stone-fronted **Victoria Terrace**. Next comes **Waterloo Place**, one of the most characteristic of all the terraces, and the semicircular-ended **Brunswick Terrace**, terminating the Georgian development. **St John's church** (2) is good Victorian Gothic of 1850.

Retrace your steps to the Jubilee Clock and continue along the Esplanade. The Royal Hotel on the right, in the Renaissance style of the late 1890s, replaced a beautiful Georgian building. Beyond this is the **Gloucester Hotel** (see above). The **statue of George III** (3) standing appropriately at the centre of the front, was erected in 1810 to mark his golden jubilee. It is of Coade stone and depicts the king in coronation robes. The statue and the symbols surrounding it were very well painted in 1949. Note the arms of Hanover in the centre of the royal arms. Bow-windowed, semicircular houses form an effective background to the statue. Further along the front is the **Royal Dorset Yacht Club**, a handsome building with Ionic columns. At the corner of Alexandra Gardens is a statue of Sir Henry Edwards, MP for the borough and a great benefactor of the town. **Pulteney** and **Devonshire Buildings** (4) are handsome terraces just before the Pier. The Esplanade ends at the **Pavilion** (5) and the Quay railway station. Ships sail from here to the Channel Islands.

Turn round here and follow the railway line along the Quay, an interesting walk with delightful views across the harbour to the Georgian terraces beyond. In St Mary Street, just before the Town Bridge, are the fine Classical **Guildhall** (1836-7) and a notable Methodist church. In St Edmund Street is the old **Golden Lion** inn, with a striking sign. Up St Mary's Street is **St Mary's church**,

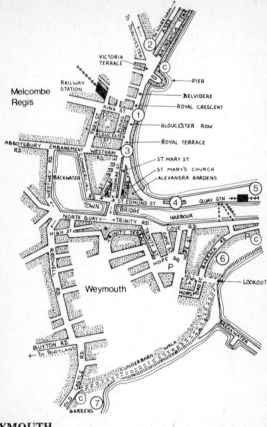

WEYMOUTH

1. Jubilee Clock
2. St John's church
3. Statue of George III
4. Pulteney and Devonshire Buildings
5. Pavilion
6. Nothe Gardens
7. Sandsfoot Castle

the parish church of Melcombe Regis (1815-17). Designed by a local architect, James Hamilton, it is a typical Georgian city church without tower or spire. Its golden cupola, surmounted by a golden ball, is a prominent Weymouth landmark (plate 1). On the inner east wall is a very fine picture of the Last Supper, painted by Sir James Thornhill, a native of Weymouth and MP for the borough in 1721. Further along the street is the seventeenth-century **Black Dog** inn, which must have been on the fringe of the country before the terraces were built along the front.

Walk 2: The Old Town of Weymouth

Take the car from King Street car park and turn left (one-way street) into Park Street, then second left into Westham Road and shortly right into St Thomas Street, leading to the Town Bridge. Overlooking this is **Trinity Church**, a pre-Victorian Gothic revival building in the Perpendicular style, good for its date. Turn left after crossing the bridge into Trinity Road, with harbour on the left, and right into Trinity Street, where there are two Tudor stone-fronted houses, the **Old Rooms** inn with projecting porch, where assemblies used to be held during the eighteenth century, and Nos. 2 and 5 (open Wednesdays and Saturdays 2.30 p.m. to 5 p.m.). Then turn left into **Hope Square**, the name derived from its being on the site of an 'ope' or creek from the harbour. It is the centre of Weymouth's brewing industry. Park your car here.

Turn up St Leonard's Road at the south-west corner of Hope Square, left into Herbert Place, right into Hartlebury Terrace and so into **Trinity Terrace**. This has charming little Georgian houses with bow windows, which overlook the harbour and Melcombe Regis beyond. This walk can be continued to Dorset Terrace and Chapelhay Street into **High Street**, the old original main street of Weymouth. The old **Town Hall** dates from the sixteenth century and looks like a humble little village church.

Walk 3. Leave Hope Square by a path on the east side named Hill Lane: this leads on to a street named Look Out. (Here is a turn left on to the Jubilee Walk, leading to the **Nothe Gardens** (6) and old fort, with magnificent views over the bay on one side and to Portland on the other. Across the bay are the white cliffs of Lulworth, and on clear days St Aldhelm's Head can be seen. There is a car park for those coming by car from Hope Square, via Horsford Street and Barrack Road.)

By turning right at Look Out one takes the Underbarn Walk to Sandsfoot Castle, about three quarters of a mile. There are fine views of the Portland Roads and breakwater and the Chesil Beach. The path emerges into Old Castle Road, where turn left. A little further on is **Sandsfoot Castle** (7), with a beautiful water garden in front. The castle was built by Henry VIII in 1539, one of a series from Kent to Cornwall, when invasion by France and Spain was expected. It was built partly of Portland stone, and partly of recognisable medieval fragments probably from Bindon Abbey, near Wool, then recently dissolved. Sandsfoot and its opposite, Portland Castle (see below), were together able to prevent hostile vessels from entering Portland Roads. Unfortunately it has been robbed of much ashlar facing-stone, and the octagonal gun-room has fallen over the cliff into the sea. The barrack building and gateway tower are left, and the Department of the Environment has completed some repairs.

In the neighbourhood. Portland, a rocky peninsula connected with the mainland only by the nine-mile long Chesil Beach, was compared by Hardy to Gibraltar. The road from Weymouth runs through Wyke Regis, and alongside the Chesil Beach. **Portland Castle**, a perfect Henry VIII fort like Sandsfoot (see above) is just off the road left, at **Castletown**. Ascend a steep hill through **Fortuneswell**, capital of Portland. The famous Portland stone quarries, some still in use, provided stone for the Banqueting Hall at Whitehall (by Inigo Jones), St Paul's Cathedral and other City churches by Christopher Wren and many other buildings. **St George's church** (1771) in the village of **Reforne**, is a perfect Georgian church with original furniture. **Church Ope Cove**, on the east side, has Portland's only trees, among which are the ruins of its oldest church. **Rufus Castle**, said to have been built by William Rufus, stands on a rocky crag. **Pennsylvania Castle** (now an hotel) is a castellated mansion built by Wyatt in 1800 for John Penn, Governor of Portland and grandson of the Quaker founder of Pennsylvania. **St Andrew's church**, further south, on the way down to Portland Bill and lighthouse, was built in 1879 to commemorate a tragic collision between the ships *Avalanche* and *Forest*. **St Peter's church, The Grove**, north from Pennsylvania Castle, is beautifully built and has been decorated by convicts from the former prison (now a Borstal). The mosaic floors were made by women from another prison.

Abbotsbury, a charming village where the Chesil Beach and Fleet estuary begin, is noted for its Swannery, first mentioned in 1393, its interesting church and the great Abbey Barn, 272 feet long. St Catherine's Chapel was a lighthouse in medieval times.

Wimborne Minster

History. Wimborne Minster is a pleasant market town, known to have been inhabited since Roman times and to have been important in the Saxon period. Saints Cuthberga and Cwenburh, sisters of the Saxon king Ina, established a nunnery at Wimborne in the early eighth century. In 871 King Alfred was at Wimborne for the funeral of his brother King Ethelred, killed fighting the Danes.

In the Middle Ages there was a flourishing wool trade and various schools and colleges were founded, including a grammar school founded by the mother of Henry VII and re-established by a royal charter under Queen Elizabeth I (though it is now a modern building).

The Duke of Monmouth was captured near Wimborne after the Battle of Sedgemoor.

The town is now a centre for agriculture, market gardening and light industries.

Approach from the east by A31 and go ahead from Leigh Road into East Street (or from Bournemouth by A349 turn left into East Street); the GPO is on the left. Take the first turn right, opposite telephone kiosks and conveniences, into Park Lane, and the car park is on the left.

Walk. Walk back into East Street and turn right; cross two branches of the river Allen or Wym, and the second turn right (footpath) leads to the **Minster** (1). Dedicated to St Cuthberga, this possibly stands on the site of the old nunnery, but the oldest part of the present building dates from the early twelfth century. The outside is a chequer-work of grey and brown stone. It has two towers, the central one being Norman (c. 1120), with pinnacles added later, and the west or bell tower Perpendicular. On the north side of the bell tower is the quarter-jack, a sixteenth-century wooden figure, now dressed as a British grenadier of Wellington's time, who strikes the bells on either side of him at each quarter-hour.

The fourteenth-century north porch has a vaulted roof and a parvise, or priest's room, above it. The nave has eight richly ornamented Transitional-Norman arches on massive pillars and two smaller plain arches. There is a brass lectern (1623) and, near the nineteenth-century pulpit, a chained book by Bishop Jewel (1614). Under the western tower is a Norman font of Purbeck marble, and on the south wall an orrery, or astronomical clock, with earth in the centre and sun and moon revolving round it, thought to have been made by Peter Lightfoot of Glastonbury in 1320, and still working. Its mechanism also works the quarter-jack.

The north transept is mainly Norman and has a newel stairway to the tower. There is an altar-recess with wall-paintings. The south transept is Early English. In the chancel, there are two

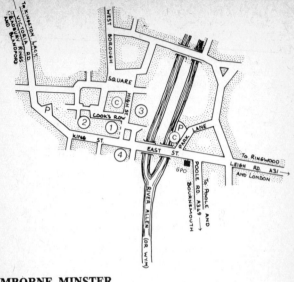

WIMBORNE MINSTER

1. Minster
2. Model Town
3. Priest's House Museum
4. Dean Court

flights of steps up to the altar. The east window has three lancets, with plate-tracery above, and the glass of the middle lancet, representing the Tree of Jesse, is fifteenth-century Belgian work. The altar rails are benches of Cromwellian date, covered with 'houseling cloths'. Just inside the rails is a fifteenth-century brass to King Ethelred, believed to have been buried here. There are several interesting tombs, including one with alabaster effigies of John Beaufort, Duke of Somerset, grandson of John of Gaunt and grandfather of Henry VII, with his wife. Underneath the chancel is a beautiful vaulted crypt.

In the south choir aisle is the curious tomb of Anthony Ettricke, recorder of Poole, who committed the Duke of Monmouth for trial. Saying that he would be buried neither inside the Minster nor outside, neither in the ground, nor above it, he had his own coffin made and inserted under an arch in the wall. He even put the expected date of his death, 1693, but as he lived another ten years, it had to be altered to 1703.

Above the vestry is the muniment room, containing many interesting medieval documents and a chained library of seventeenth-century books.

West of the Minster, off West Road, is a one in ten **model of the town** (2), showing all the interesting buildings, both back and front. From the Model Town, turn back along Cook's Row and left into High Street. The **Priest's House Museum** (3), sixteenth-century, on the right (open weekdays, May to September) contains objects of local interest from prehistoric times onwards.

Go on into the Square, and from the north-west of this into **West Borough**, in which there are some fine Georgian houses. Return down High Street, and just opposite where it comes out into East Street is **Dean Court**, another fine house (4), dating from 1725.

In the neighbourhood. Leave by the Blandford Road (B3082). About half a mile out of the town, on the left, is the thirteenth-century **St Margaret's Hospital**, formerly a leper hospital, now a chapel and almshouse. A little further on, again on the left, is **Kingston Lacy**, the beautiful park and house of the Bankes family of Corfe Castle. It is open to the public and has a magnificent collection of pictures and sculpture.

Further along, on the right, are the Iron Age earthworks of **Badbury Rings**.

About one mile south of Wimborne, along the Poole road is **Canford Magna**. The mansion, formerly the seat of Lord Wimborne, is now Canford School. It is mainly of nineteenth-century date, but has a fifteenth-century kitchen. There is an extremely interesting church, mainly of the Saxon and Norman periods, the Saxon nave having become the chancel of the Norman church.

TOWNS OF HAMPSHIRE

Aldershot

History. There are records of life in the Aldershot district from King Alfred's time, but the town only grew up after the establishment of the first camp by the War Department in 1853. From that time it expanded very rapidly and since 1961 the 'Home of the British Army' has been almost entirely rebuilt and vastly improved.

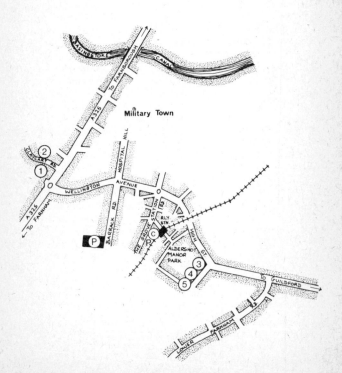

ALDERSHOT

1. Royal Garrison Church
2. Statue of Wellington
3. Manor House

4. Heroes' Garden and Shrine
5. St Michael's church

Approach by A325 from Farnborough. Cross the Basingstoke Canal, and about one mile on, on the right, is the **Royal Garrison Church** (1), rich in military history and memorials. Just short of this, Claycart Road leads to a mound on which is a fine equestrian **statue of the Duke of Wellington** (2), moved from London in 1885. At the roundabout, just beyond the Garrison Church, turn left into Wellington Avenue. The army town is mainly on the left and the civilian town on the right. After about three quarters of a mile, turn right at a roundabout into Station Road. This leads into The Grove, where there is a car park. (There is also a multi-storey car park off Barrack Road.)

Walk. From the car park walk eastwards, crossing the railway, into Aldershot Manor Park. At the far side of this is the old **Manor House** (1670), now the registrar's office (3). Just south of this are the **Heroes' Garden** and **Heroes' Shrine**, war memorials, including a large Portland-stone figure of Christ stilling the storm, and a rockery made from stones in 'blitzed' towns (4). The **parish church of St Michael** (5) dates originally from the twelfth century, when it was a 'chapel of ease' to Crondall. The Lady Chapel is the oldest part, and the brick tower fifteenth-century. The church was much enlarged and restored in the nineteenth and early twentieth centuries. There are some fascinating monuments to the Tichborne and White families, and some good woodwork.

Alresford

History. Alresford belonged to the Bishops of Winchester from an early date. Bishop Godfrey de Lucy (1189-1204) re-established an old market there and also built a dam on the Itchen, between the town and Old Alresford village. A reservoir of 200 acres was formed. The Bishop intended to make the Itchen navigable from Southampton to Alresford, but did not succeed. In the seventeenth and eighteenth centuries the town had several disastrous fires and was almost entirely rebuilt after one in 1736, so that it consists largely of very attractive houses of the early Georgian period.

Approach by East Street (A31) from Alton. Car parking is allowed in Broad Street, a very wide tree-lined street leading down to the dam or 'Great Weir'.

Walk down Broad Street, noticing, among many charming houses, **No. 27** on the west side (1), where Mary Russell Mitford, authoress of *Our Village*, was born in 1787. There is a fourteenth-century bridge leading to the dam, but it can only be seen from a private garden. Sixty acres of the original reservoir remain. Return to the

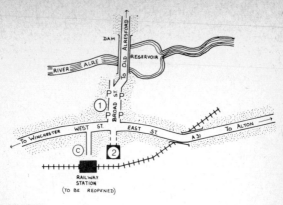

ALRESFORD

1. Mary Russell Mitford's birthplace

2. Church of St John the Baptist

top of Broad Street, and where it meets East Street and West Street a passage leads through to the **church**, St John the Baptist (2). Rebuilt, except for the tower, after a fire in 1694, it was again largely rebuilt, in Perpendicular style, in 1897-8. It has two weathered Saxon roods in the north and west faces of the medieval lower part of the tower.

Alton

History. Alton is a pleasant town in the hop-growing district of Hampshire. It had a church in Norman times, and returned two MPs to Edward I's parliament. In the Civil War it saw heavy fighting, and Colonel Boles, for the King, made a famous and heroic stand in St Lawrence's church against Waller's vastly superior forces. Boles and nearly all his men were killed. When the war was over, Alton became a peaceful little manufacturing town, beer being the chief product, another being a coarse material, mentioned by both Gilbert White and Cobbett as baracan or barragoon.

Approach Alton from the north-east by A31, driving along the main street until it becomes High Street. On the right, opposite the GPO and by the fire station, turn into Cross and Pillory Lane, which leads to a large car park.

47

Walk. Return to High Street. On the corner is the handsome **Midland Bank** (1), and there are many other good houses in the street, including numbers 4, 6 and 8. On the south-east side are the **Swan** hotel (2), late eighteenth or early nineteenth century, but of old origin, and the **Curtis Museum** (3) (open weekdays 2 p.m. to 5 p.m., Saturdays 10 a.m. to 1 p.m. and 2 p.m. to 5 p.m., closed

ALTON

1. Midland Bank
2. Swan hotel
3. Curtis Museum

4. St Lawrence's church
5. Geale Almshouses
6. Friends' Meeting House
7. Eggar's Grammar School

Sundays, Wednesdays and bank holidays), including interesting exhibits of brewing implements, dolls' houses, fire insurance marks and Victoriana.

On the left in Church Street is **St Lawrence's church** (4). It has a font which may be Saxon, and a Norman central tower with four massive arches and wonderful carved capitals. Most of the church is Perpendicular. On one of the pillars are some fifteenth-century wall-paintings and on the same pillar is a memorial brass to Colonel Boles. Bullet marks from his fight still show on the south door. The church has many other treasures. Nearly opposite are the **Geale Almshouses** (1653) (5). Further along Church Street on the right, is the **Friends' Meeting House** (c. 1672) (6). **Eggar's Grammar School**, further along the main street eastward, dates partly from the sixteenth century (7). The famous **Treloar Hospital** is at the other end of the town.

In the neighbourhood. Chawton (turn left off the Winchester road at the second roundabout) was Jane Austen's home from 1809 to 1817. Here she wrote *Emma* and *Persuasion*. The house is now a museum, open daily.

Selborne, about five miles south of Alton on the Petersfield road, is a charming village, made famous by Gilbert White's *Natural History*. White was vicar there for many years, until his death in 1793. His house, The Wakes, is a museum. He made the zigzag path up the beech-clad hill, Selborne Hanger. His grave, just north of the church, is marked simply 'G. W., 26th June 1793', but in the church is a beautiful modern window in his memory, showing St Francis of Assisi with many of the birds and animals mentioned in the *Natural History of Selborne*.

Andover

History. Andover was known in Saxon times, and is the traditional site of the first payment of Danegeld by Ethelred the Unready to Olaf the Dane. In the Domesday survey six mills are recorded in Andover. It was a flourishing wool town in medieval times, and became a corporate borough under King John. Charles I stayed the night at the Star and Garter after a skirmish with Parliamentary forces in the Civil War. The vicar, a Royalist, was later driven out by the Roundheads and is said to have escaped along the roofs of East Street, carrying the church plate. James II stayed, possibly at the Angel inn, on his way to meet the forces of William of Orange but while there he was told that his cause was hopeless and decided to abdicate.

Andover was extremely busy in the coaching period, being on

the main road from London to Salisbury and the west.

A Royal Air Force establishment was set up in Andover in 1916, and in 1955 the RAF received the freedom of the borough, to mark the long connection between the two. Andover is now an expanding town with vast developments of housing and industry.

Approach. Enter by London Road. Turn right into East Street and the car park is on the left.

Walk. Turn back down East Street and right into London Street. The **Star and Garter** hotel (1), on the right at the south-east corner of Market Place, has a Regency front with good bow windows. Cross over into Bridge Street and, after crossing the bridge over the river Anton, turn right into Western Avenue. The picturesque old **Town Mill** (2) is being restored as a youth centre. Turn right into Chantry Street, and right again for **St Mary's church** (3) on the left. This is a fine example of the Early English thirteenth-century style, though it was built c. 1846 on the site of a medieval

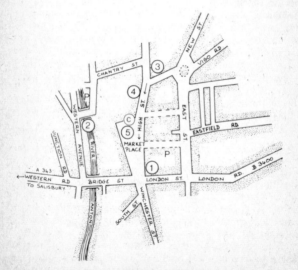

ANDOVER

1. Star and Garter hotel
2. Town Mill
3. St Mary's church
4. Angel inn
5. Town Hall

church which had been condemned by an architect as unsafe but proved to be so strong that gunpowder was needed for its demolition. The churchyard is said to be haunted by an invisible man of whom, however, just one black-stockinged leg can be seen! A fine Norman doorway from the old church forms the High Street entrance to the churchyard. Further down, on the right, is the **Angel** (4), Andover's oldest inn. Proceed down High Street into the Market Place. The **Town Hall** (5) is a handsome Classical building (1825).

In the neighbourhood. Enham Alamein, two miles north, is a rehabilitation centre for soldiers of both world wars.

Wherwell, about three miles south-east, is one of Hampshire's most beautiful villages, set in the lovely scenery of the Test valley.

Basingstoke

History. Basingstoke, now a large industrial town of nearly 60,000 inhabitants, with a fine modern town centre, was inhabited before Roman times. It was a royal manor in Saxon times. Henry III granted a charter in 1227, and a charter of James I (1623) still survives. A medieval cloth industry has given place to others.

Approach. From the M3 or A30 carefully follow signs for town centre and multi-storey car park. This is over the middle of the new town centre, and from it pathways and steps lead down into Church Street, part of the old town.

Walk. The **parish church**, St Michael (1), is mainly Perpendicular, though the north chapel, by Sir Charles Nicholson, is a memorial of the First World War. The church contains royal arms of Elizabeth I, James I and William III, and an Elizabethan alms box (1576). Bomb damage from the Second World War can be seen on the outer east wall. West of the church is **Church Cottage** (2), probably sixteenth-century and listed for preservation. North of the railway, in a cemetery on the right on Chapel Hill, are the ruins of the **Holy Ghost Chapel**, built by Bishop Fox in 1525, but originally thirteenth-century, and the **Holy Trinity Chapel** (1542) (3). It is said that parts of the ruins were blown up, as a schoolboy prank, by Gilbert White, the Selborne naturalist, and his schoolfellows.

Return to Church Street. Near the south end is Cross Street, leading into New Street, where the **Willis Museum and Art Gallery** (1930) (4) contains much of local historical interest and a fine collection of clocks and watches. The **Town Hall** (1832) (5) is in the Market Place near the site of the original Mote Hall. In London Road are the **James Deane Almshouses** (1607) (6). Here turn down

Hackwood Road and right into Southern Road. On the corner of Victoria Street is **All Saints church** (7), a very fine building of 1915-20 by the celebrated church architect, Temple Moore.

In the neighbourhood. Basing about a mile east of Basingstoke, is a charming old village with a handsome church, St Mary's, and the ruins of **Basing House** (open Saturdays, Sundays and bank holidays). The earthworks of a Norman castle remain. A magnificent Elizabethan mansion, built on the site by the first Marquess of Winchester, was heroically held for the King during the Civil War for over two years by John Paulet, fifth Marquess, but was finally taken by Cromwell himself and completely destroyed. The church has several Paulet monuments and other interesting features.

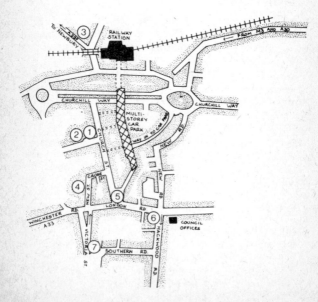

BASINGSTOKE

1. Parish church of St Michael
2. Church Cottage
3. Ruined chapels
4. Willis Museum and Art Gallery
5. Town Hall
6. James Deane Almshouses
7. All Saints' church

Silchester, about six miles north, was the Roman *Calleva Atrebatum* and probably a Celtic town before that. Impressive parts of the Roman walls still remain. Excavations revealed, among much else of interest, the foundations of a fourth-century Roman Christian church. There is a small museum on Silchester Common, but most of the finds are in Reading Museum. The village church, of Norman origin, is just within the Roman walls.

Bishop's Waltham

History. The history of Bishop's Waltham dates back to the Bronze Age; pit dwellings, burial sites including the Wessex bell barrow in Shore Lane, flint implements, pottery and other relics have been found. The Romans and Saxons also occupied the site. *Wealdham* was the Saxon name, and the prefix 'Bishop's' was added in 904, when the Bishop of Winchester acquired land there from Edward the Elder. The Danes destroyed the place in 1001, but in Norman times it was flourishing again. Bishop Henri de Blois built a fortified palace there and many kings visited it, including Henry II, who held a council there to organise a crusade. William of Wykeham often lived there and died there in 1204. Unfortunately the palace was besieged by the Roundheads and seriously damaged in the Civil War, and Bishop Curll, a Royalist, is said to have had to escape in a dung-cart when the palace fell.

Bishop's Waltham is now a prosperous little market town with several industries, including flour-milling.

Approach. Entering by A333 from Winchester, turn left at the roundabout into B3035, and sharp right at the junction of Lower Lane and Brook Street; the car park is on the right.

Walk. Cross Brook Street, and turn left up St Peter's Street for the **parish church** (1). This is mainly a nineteenth-century restoration on the site of former churches, but has a sixteenth-century tower, a Norman font, a fine Jacobean pulpit, eighteenth-century west gallery and some other interesting features. Return down St Peter's Street and High Street, in which are several pleasant old houses, including the Georgian **Barclay's Bank** (2).

Cross St George's Square to the **Palace** (3) (open March and April, weekdays 9.30 a.m. to 5.30 p.m., Sundays 2 p.m. to 5.30 p.m.; May to September, weekdays 9.30 a.m. to 7 p.m., Sundays 2 p.m. to 7 p.m.; October, weekdays 9.30 a.m. to 5.30 p.m., Sundays 2 p.m. to 5.30 p.m.; November to February, weekdays 9.30 a.m. to 4 p.m., Sundays 2 p.m. to 4 p.m.; closed from 1 p.m. to 2 p.m. and on Mondays except bank holidays). Although so much has been

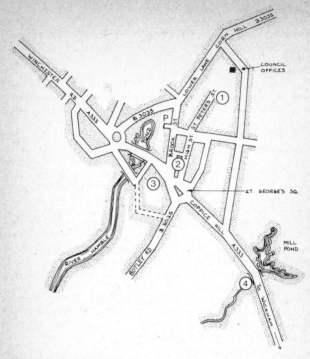

BISHOP'S WALTHAM

1. Parish church
2. Barclays Bank

3. Palace
4. Waltham Mill

destroyed, there remain the front of the great hall, probably Wykeham's work, with five windows, the foundations of an apsidal chapel, the lower stage of a tower, and some of the old domestic buildings. Round part of the site is a fifteenth-century brick wall, the work of Bishop Langton.

From the Palace, return to the square, and walk along Coppice Hill (the A333 Wickham road). About half a mile along, on the right, is **Waltham Mill** (4), one of three mills in Bishop's Waltham mentioned in the Domesday survey.

Fareham

History. Fareham is an old market town at the north-west of Portsmouth Harbour. It had a church in Saxon times, and was a Parliamentary borough from Edward I's reign. It has had a flourishing trade in the building of yachts and small boats, and similar industries.

Approach. Enter by A27 from Portsmouth. About a quarter of a mile on from the railway viaduct, turn right into High Street and then take the first turn left into Osborn Road, where there is a car park on the right at the far end. There is also a multi-storey car park near the church.

Walk. Return along Osborn Road to the **church** (SS Peter and Paul). This has Saxon long-and-short work on the north-east angle of the old chancel, which is early English and now a chapel to the new chancel (1888). There is a fourteenth-century oak reredos in the north aisle. The tower is eighteenth-century, and the nave twentieth-century by Sir Charles Nicholson.

FAREHAM

High Street is a pleasant Georgian street with some very good houses. The rest of Fareham is modern. Relief roads and pedestrian precincts are being made, and will improve the town centre.

Farnborough

History. Farnborough is mentioned in the Domesday Survey (1086) as *Ferneberga*. It became a town in the nineteenth century when Aldershot grew up after the Crimean War. In 1906 the first aircraft industry was established in Farnborough. It has now assumed vast proportions as the Royal Aircraft Establishment, and the Farnborough Air Show has become a national event.

Approach. Enter from the north by A325. Farnborough Road runs right through the middle of the town (what remains of old Farnborough lies off to the left in Farnborough Street). A little way past the Ship Inn on the left is **Farnborough Hill** (1) where the ex-empress Eugenie, wife of Napoleon III, spent her long widowhood (1873-1920). The house is now a convent school. The main car park is at the railway station, on the right.

Walk. Opposite the station, by a large white modern block called Abbey House, is the drive leading up to **St Michael's Benedictine abbey** (2), founded by Empress Eugenie. Near it, on a beautifully wooded hill, is **St Michael's church**, a fascinating building in the French 'Flamboyant' style, also built by the Empress. In the crypt (open in afternoons only; key from the abbey) the Emperor, Empress and their son, the Prince Imperial, are buried.

Continue down Farnborough Road, and left at the first roundabout into Rectory Road. The second turn right leads up to the old **parish church** (3) now much enlarged. It contains some Norman work and medieval wall-paintings, and has a timber tower and spire.

Fordingbridge

Fordingbridge, about six miles north of Ringwood, has a beautiful medieval **bridge** with seven pointed arches (1). Just short of the bridge is the recreation ground, and by the river bank is a **statue** of the artist Augustus John (2), who lived in Fordingbridge for many years. The car park is in Roundhill. The seventeenth-century **Old Manor** (3), in Salisbury Street, was formerly a court-house. **St Mary's Church** (4), south-west of the town in Church Street, has an

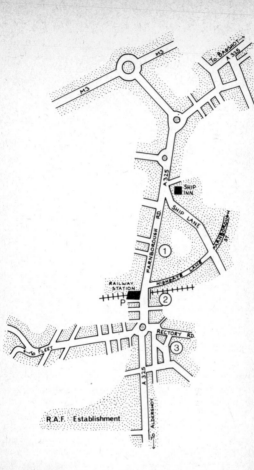

FARNBOROUGH

1. Farnborough Hill
2. St Michael's Abbey

3. Parish church

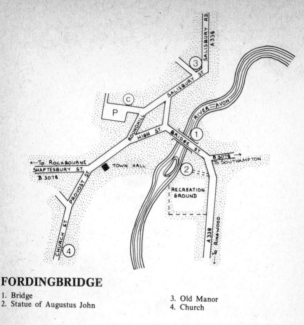

FORDINGBRIDGE

1. Bridge
2. Statue of Augustus John
3. Old Manor
4. Church

Early English chancel, decorated nave, Perpendicular tower, and a splendid, angel roof of the East Anglian type in the north chapel.

In the neighbourhood. Leave Fordingbridge by B3078 for Sandleheath, where turn right to **Rockbourne Roman villa**. About fifty rooms of this villa have been excavated, under the direction of the late Mr Morley Hewitt, who discovered it. It was probably occupied from the second century A.D. until the end of the Roman period. It includes bathrooms and mosaic pavements. There is a small museum on the site.

Gosport

History. Bishop Henri de Blois of Winchester is said to have named the little fishing village 'God's Port' when he took refuge there from a storm, c. 1150. In medieval times the town was fortified with moated ramparts, but only small sections remain.

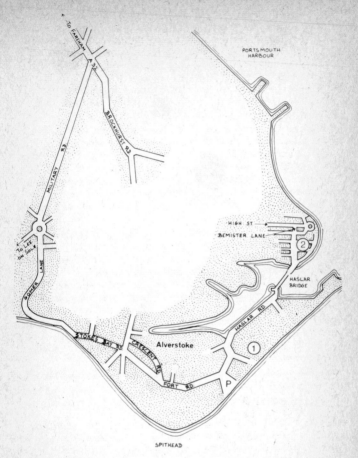

GOSPORT
1. Royal Naval Hospital

2. Holy Trinity church

Gosport grew up largely with the growth of the Royal Navy, for which it was the chief victualling station. All the services now have establishments there. It is also a centre for boat-building, yachting and other seaside amusements, and includes the seaside resorts of Stokes Bay and Lee-on-the-Solent. Throughout her reign Queen Victoria always travelled by train to Gosport to embark for the Isle of Wight. The railway station (1842) is now disused, but it will be preserved. It was designed by Sir William Tite and has a magnificent Tuscan colonnade.

Approach. The road approach is from Fareham by A32. After about three miles leave A32 and bear right into Military Road. At a roundabout go on into Gomer Lane, and turn left at the end of this into Stokes Bay Road. The second turn left leads into Anglesey Road, and the first turn right into **Crescent Road**, **Alverstoke**. This is a fine Georgian crescent and the best street in Gosport. From here drive on into Fort Road. About half a mile along on the right is a car park.

Walk. Walk along Haslar Road. The **Royal Naval Hospital** (1), a handsome building founded in George II's time, is on the right. Cross the bridge over Haslar Lake. In Trinity Green, just beyond the bridge on the right, is **Holy Trinity church** (2), dating originally from 1696, but partly rebuilt and enlarged in the nineteenth century. In it is an organ which once belonged to the Duke of Chandos of Canons Park, Middlesex, and was often used by Handel when composing. Cross South Street, and Bemister Lane leads into **High Street**, which still has some old houses. Along the front sections of the old ramparts and the very modern developments form an interesting contrast.

Lymington

History. Lymington is an old town and port on the Solent and is within a short distance of the boundary of the New Forest. A car ferry runs across the Solent to Yarmouth, Isle of Wight, so Lymington is excellently placed for exploring both forest and island. In 1950 the borough celebrated the eight hundredth anniversary of its incorporation under a charter granted by Baldwin de Redvers, though some historians now believe that the first charter dated from 1250, but the original settlement was far older than this. About a mile north of the town is the great Iron Age camp of Buckland Rings with its triple ring of fortifications. This commanded the upper reaches of the harbour, and here the earliest inhabitants lived. Later there was a small village at the

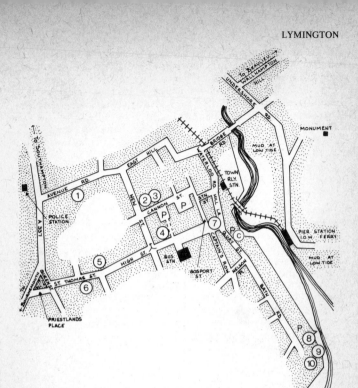

LYMINGTON

1. Town Hall
2. Community Centre
3. Library
4. Angel hotel
5. Parish church of St Thomas

6. Monmouth House
7. Quay Hill
8. Royal Lymington Yacht Club
9. Lymington Town Sailing Club
10. Bath House

lowest fordable point of the river, at the bottom of what is now Lymington High Street. All through the Middle Ages Lymington was an important port and it actually fitted out double the number of ships provided by Portsmouth for the invasion of France during the war of 1345. For many centuries the town was also noted for its salt industry, but this died out in Victorian times. During the eighteenth century the town became a popular watering-place. It is now a great yachting and boat-building centre.

Approach the town by the A357, from Southampton turning left, or from Bournemouth right, at the lights opposite the police station, into Avenue Road. Shortly after passing the new **Town Hall** (1), opened by H.M. the Queen in 1966, on the right, turn right into New Street. At the next crossroads, turn left into Cannon Street. The **Community Centre** (2) and **Library** (3) are on the left, and a car park on the right. The Community Centre is one of the earliest of its kind, having been founded soon after the Second World War. Part of it was formerly an old malt house. During the French Revolution it housed refugees. The original building has been added to judiciously and is used for all kinds of interesting activities.

Walk. From the car park take the footpath through the yard of the **Angel** hotel (4), a charming old coaching house, and turn right up High Street, which contains many Georgian houses. At the top is the **parish church of St Thomas** (5), standing very well at the west end of the street. It was originally Early English, of which there are remains in the chancel. The tower dates from 1670 and is surmounted by an eighteenth-century cupola. Inside are late eighteenth-century galleries. In 1910 the roof was restored, and some of the bosses from the old roof are in a case at the west end of the nave. Opposite the church is **Monmouth House** (6), a fine old late seventeenth-century brick building, now a home for old people. In 1685 this house belonged to the Knaptons, supporters of the Duke of Monmouth, and meetings of his followers were held there.

From this point turn back and walk down High Street. As one descends the hill there is a good view of the **monument** to the distinguished sailor Sir Harry Burrard Neale, Bart., RN, on the far side of the harbour. At the bottom of the hill cross the road and walk down **Quay Hill** (7) (footpath only), which contains some charming old houses. Turn right into Quay Street, which leads through a very narrow lane with many antique shops, one of which has a female figurehead. This street emerges on to the north end of the quay. Along the quay are seats from which one can watch the hundreds of yachts and boats of all descriptions. At the south end of the quay, about half a mile away, are the **Royal Lymington Yacht Club** (8), the **Lymington Town Sailing Club** (9) and the sea-water baths with **Bath House** (10) dating from 1833. Near the Royal Lymington Yacht Club house is a gas lamp on a Doric column, erected in 1832 to commemorate the lighting of the town by gas: 'a tribute of respect and gratitude to Sir Harry Neale, Bart., RN for his munificent gift of the iron columns for the public lamps'.

Travellers who are not good walkers could return to the car park from High Street, drive down Cannon Street, right into Gosport Street, across the bottom of High Street into Captain's Row, a charming old street, left down Nelson Place, and either left along Quay Street, or right along Bath Road, to the car parks on the quay.

In the neighbourhood. Beaulieu is five miles north-east of Lymington. (Leave the town by Bridge Road and turn left and then right.) **Beaulieu Abbey** was founded by King John in 1204 for Cistercian monks. After the Dissolution the great abbey church, a magnificent building, was demolished, and the stones used for building coastal forts. The monks' refectory, a noble thirteenth-century building, is now the **parish church**, and contains a very fine pulpit. The former gateway to the abbey is now **Palace House**, the seat of Lord Montagu of Beaulieu. The famous **motor museum** is in the grounds.

Two miles to the south of Beaulieu is **Buckler's Hard**, a most attractive village and formerly a busy shipbuilding yard. Many of the famous wooden warships of Nelson's time were built there. There is an interesting **maritime museum**.

Lyndhurst

History. Lyndhurst, the capital of the New Forest, and a good centre for exploring it, was already a royal manor in A.D. 980. It was given to Amesbury Abbey, Wiltshire, by the Saxon queen Elfrida. The 'Queen's House', first recorded as being built in 1300, was a royal residence for several centuries, and was occupied by many kings and queens, the last king to stay there being George III, on his way to Weymouth in 1789. Fanny Burney records this visit, and the loyalty of the people of Lyndhurst, very amusingly in her diary. The Forest laws have been administered here throughout the centuries.

Approach. Coming from Southampton by A35, turn left into the Brockenhurst-Lymington road, and shortly right into the car park. Coming from Winchester or Bournemouth, keep to the right-hand lane in Lyndhurst High Street and turn right into the car park.

Walk. From the car park, turn left up High Street. The **parish church of St Michael and All Angels** (1), which replaced a charming Georgian church in 1863, stands on an artificial mound, possibly a site of pagan worship. The church is a veritable museum of Victoriana, including windows by Burne-Jones, William Morris, Kemp and others, a fine fresco behind the altar of the parable of

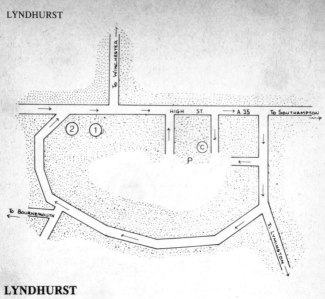

LYNDHURST

1. Parish church   2. Queen's House

the ten virgins, by Lord Leighton, and carved angels with musical instruments. Mrs Hargreaves, original of *Alice in Wonderland*, is buried in the churchyard.

Close to the church is the **Queen's House** (King's House when the reigning monarch is a king). This charming brick building (2) incorporates the offices of the Forestry Commission, and the Verderers Court of the New Forest. The **Verderer's Hall** is partly Tudor, c. 1530, with fine Tudor chimney-stacks. It contains some interesting furniture and relics of the New Forest's fascinating history, much of which can be discovered here. The rest of the building dates mainly from the Stuart period.

Odiham

History. Odiham (plate 7) is an old and very charming market town between Aldershot and Basingstoke. Odiham Castle, about one mile away from the town and approached by various side-roads west of the village of North Warnborough, is thought to

1. The parish church of St Mary, Melcombe Regis, Weymouth, designed by James Hamilton, and built in 1815-17.

2. Blandford Forum, looking towards the Market Place, Town Hall and church.

3. Christchurch Priory is now the parish church. The tower dates from the fifteenth century.

4. *Gold Hill, Shaftesbury. On the right is the wall of the abbey precincts.*

5. *The medieval stone bridge over the Stour at Sturminster Newton.*

6. One of five inscribed stones, dating from the seventh and eighth centuries, in the church of Lady St Mary, Wareham.

7. An old street in Odiham, one of the most delightful small towns of Hampshire.

8. *The Market Place at Romsey, with the statue of Lord Palmerston, and the Abbey Church behind.*

9. *This cannon stands beside H.M.S. Victory in Portsmouth Dockyard.*

10. *Winchester Cathedral; the west front.*

11. The West gate, Winchester's only major gate to survive.

Map showing the towns and cities described in this book.

Crick

● Malmesbury

Wootton Bassett ●

● Chippenham

Corsham ●   ● Calne

● Melksham

Bradford-
on-Avon   ● Devize

● Trowbridge

● Westbury

● Warminster

WILTSHIRE

Wilton

Shaftesbury ●

Sherborne ●

Sturminster ●
Newton

● Blandford Forum

● Beaminster   **DORSET**

Wimborne ●
Minster

● Bridport

Bournemou
Poole ●

Lyme
Regis

● Dorchester

Wareham ●

Swanage

● Weymouth

Swindon

● Marlborough

0 3 6 9 12 15 18
Miles

Farnborough ●
Basingstoke ●   Aldershot ●
                    Odiham
● Whitchurch

Andover ●

HAMPSHIRE
                              ● Alton

                    ● Alresford

Salisbury
            Winchester ●

                              Petersfield ●

● Romsey

            ● Bishops Waltham

Fordingbridge
            Southampton

Ringwood   ● Lyndhurst
                    ● Fareham

Lymington   Gosport ●
Christchurch   Portsmouth

Isle of Wight

12. The Arcades of the town wall at Southampton.

13. The Saxon church at Bradford-on-Avon, founded by St Aldhelm in 705.

14. *The Yelde Hall, or old town hall, in The Shambles at Chippenham.*

15. *The Green at Calne, surrounded by the Georgian houses of cloth-merchants.*

16. The Market Cross at Malmesbury.

17. (Opposite) Marlborough's broad High Street, scene of the
Mop Fair in October.

18. The statue of William III in the Square at Petersfield.

19. The Market Cross at Devizes has an inscription recounting the story of Ruth Pierce.

20. *The Railway Museum at Swindon contains several locomotives of the Great Western Railway. It was formerly a chapel.*

21. *The tomb in Trowbridge churchyard of Thomas Helliker, an executed cloth-worker.*

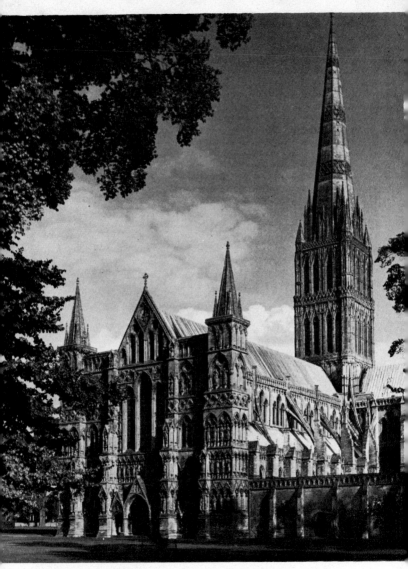

22. *Salisbury Cathedral, renowned for its Early English architecture and its lofty spire.*

have been a royal residence of the kings of Wessex. The Normans built a castle soon after the Conquest, and King John is known to have stayed there. An octagonal tower, the shell of which is all that now remains, probably dates from a little later. In 1216 the castle was besieged by Louis, Dauphin of France. The young Prince Edward was imprisoned there by Simon de Montfort in 1265, and another royal prisoner, in the next century, was King David of Scotland.

Approach from the east by A287 and drive a little way up High Street. This is very wide and parking is allowed on the south side.

Walk. Walk up and down High Street, which is full of beautiful houses, including **Marycourt** (1), of dark brick with a lovely shell-hood over the door. The **George** hotel (2) has a Georgian front, but is partly sixteenth-century. **The Priory**, at the far end, formerly the vicarage (3), is partly Queen Anne and partly Tudor.

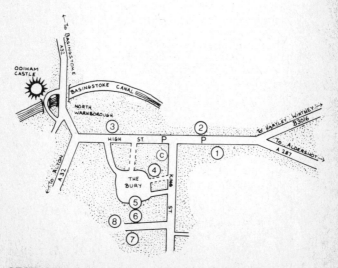

ODIHAM

1. Marycourt
2. George hotel
3. The Priory
4. House of cob

5. Stocks and whipping-post
6. All Saints' church
7. Almshouses
8. Pest House

King Street, on the south side of High Street, leads into a square called **The Bury**, where there are several more charming houses including one of cob (4). Outside the churchyard are the old **stocks** and **whipping-post** (5). The **church**, All Saints (6), is large and imposing. Though restored about 1897, it has some Decorated and Perpendicular work and a good brick Classical tower dated 1647. Its treasures include a Norman pillar piscina, a thirteenth-century font, several brasses, royal arms of Charles II (1660) and galleries with good staircases and balustrades.

South of the church are some charming brick **almshouses** (1623) (7), and in the south-west corner of the churchyard is the old **Pest House** (8).

Petersfield

History. Flint tools found in the district show that there was probably human life at Petersfield as long ago as the Middle Stone Age. A large group of Bronze Age burial mounds of various types, on the Heath, prove that it was inhabited from before 1000 B.C. Later the district, with its good soil and the downs nearby, had a flourishing agricultural and sheep and cattle-farming industry. The Romans had a villa at Stroud, just outside Petersfield.

In early medieval times, various charters for markets and fairs were granted to the town, including one still existing granted by John in 1198, the year before he became king. Two members of Parliament were returned in 1306. In the early seventeenth-century there was a cloth and leather industry employing about a thousand people. In the coaching period Petersfield was an important posting centre on the London-Portsmouth road, and had a great many inns. It is now a cheerful market town and residential district, with good opportunities for education and music. Its musical festival, started in 1901, has had many famous conductors.

Approach by A3 (the London-Portsmouth road). After coming down Ramshill and passing on the left the council offices, formerly **Old College**, a handsome early Georgian building (1), keep straight on into Station Road and turn left into a car park.

Walk. A passage leads from the car park into the Square or Market Place, where there is a fine equestrian **statue of William III** (2). He had no special connection with Petersfield, but the statue (plate 18) was given by Sir William Joliffe MP, who admired him. A very charming old timber-framed house stands on the north-west corner of the Square (3). The **church**, St Peter's (4), south of the Square, was originally Norman, with two towers. The

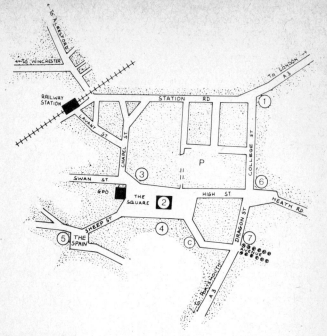

PETERSFIELD

1. Old College
2. Statue of William III
3. Timber-framed house
4. St Peter's church

5. John Goodyer's house
6. Red Lion
7. Dragon House

chancel arch, formerly part of the central tower, is of rich Norman work. Towards the end of the twelfth century the nave received aisles and a west tower was added. There is a fifteenth-century font and a few other old features, but the greater part of the church was 'restored' in Victorian times.

Sheep Street, south-west of the Square, has some sixteenth-century timber-framed cottages and some eighteenth-century houses. It leads into **The Spain**, which also has some very handsome Georgian houses, and an earlier house which belonged to

John Goodyer, the celebrated botanist (1592-1664); it has a memorial tablet, but has been refronted, altering its character (5). (The names Sheep Street and The Spain are probably connected with the former wool-trade with Spain.)

Return to the Square and cross it into High Street, which has some pleasant old houses on both sides. At the far end, across the A3 in Heath Road, is the **Red Lion** hotel (6), with eighteenth-century front, but partly dating from much earlier. Heath Road leads to the very pretty lake and the Heath with its tumuli. Return to the Red Lion, and turn left down Dragon Street (the Portsmouth road, A3). Good houses here include **Dragon House** (7) with eighteenth-century front, but timber-framed back, and parts of the interior dating from the sixteenth century or earlier. It has a gazebo at the end of the garden, which may be seen from The Avenue.

In the neighbourhood. Just south of Petersfield, on either side of the Portsmouth road, are two high, round hills, **War Down** on the left and **Butser Hill** on the right, with extensive views southwards to the sea and the Isle of Wight. Butser has, on its spurs, some defensive earthworks of uncertain date.

Buriton, of which Petersfield was just a hamlet in early days, is a pretty village about a mile to the south, and east of the Portsmouth road. Edward Gibbon, the historian, often stayed there with his father and stepmother.

East Meon, about five miles west of Petersfield (leave by the Winchester road and turn left at Langrish) is a very charming village with a Norman church with a remarkable Tournai-marble font, which depicts the Fall of Man.

North-west of the town, on the Alresford road, is **Stoner Hill**, a very steep hill covered with beautiful trees, mainly beeches. East and south-east of Petersfield are some of the loveliest parts of West Sussex.

Portsmouth

History. The beginnings of Portsmouth's history are to be found at Portchester Castle, originally a Roman fort, which stands at the head of Portsmouth Harbour. This was the westernmost of the nine Saxon Shore forts, constructed c. A.D. 300-400, as a vast scheme of defence against Saxon pirates, and extending from Portchester to Brancaster in Norfolk. The Roman walls enclose nine acres, and fourteen of the original twenty bastions survive. The Normans placed their great keep in the north-west corner of the Roman fort, and the parish church of Portchester in the south-east corner. The Castle became an embarkation port during the thirteenth and fourteenth centuries and was visited by several monarchs.

Meanwhile a settlement was growing up at the mouth of the harbour, round the Camber, a creek forming a natural harbour. It was of sufficient importance to be granted a charter by Richard I in 1194. King John had the first dock built here. In 1338 and 1369 the town was burnt by the French. During the sixteenth century Henry VII and Henry VIII enlarged the docks, and Henry VIII built Southsea Castle, part of a chain of forts stretching from Kent to Cornwall.

Charles I's favourite, George Villiers, Duke of Buckingham, unpopular after his failure to relieve a Protestant force holding out at La Rochelle in 1627, was stabbed as he was leaving his house in Portsmouth High Street by a disgruntled officer named Felton. Felton was executed and his remains were gibbeted on Southsea Common. During the Civil War the town was garrisoned for the Royalists by Colonel George Goring. Closely pressed by the Parliamentary forces, he threatened to blow up the powder magazine in the Square Tower and so devastate the old town, unless he were granted honourable terms for surrender, to which the Parliamentary commander agreed.

After the Restoration in 1660 Charles II employed a Dutch engineer, Sir Bernard de Gomme, to carry out a vast scheme of refortification, which continued for several decades. The town of Portsea, the dockyard to the north of old Portsmouth, and Gosport on the far side of the harbour, were also fortified. By the 1870s these fortifications became redundant, and were levelled, except for the most interesting works of various dates alongside the entrance to the harbour at Old Portsmouth. During the 1860s, fearing an invasion by Napoleon III of France, Lord Palmerston, then Prime Minister, built along Portsdown Ridge a series of forts known as 'Pam's Folly', as well as four remarkable island forts at Spithead.

From the eighteenth century onwards the history of Portsmouth is practically that of the Royal Navy. Bad food and brutal discipline, as well as the wicked custom of the press-gang, caused mutiny to break out in 1797, but fortunately the trouble was soon settled. Nelson started on his last voyage from Portsmouth in October 1805. Many charming and interesting old houses were destroyed in the bombardment of 1940. The handsome Victorian Guildhall (1886-90) was also burnt out, but has been completely restored. During the nineteenth century, Southsea was developed as a watering-place. With its wide common and beautiful views across Spithead to the Isle of Wight, it soon became very popular, especially for officers' wives and families.

Approach. Enter the city through the suburb of Cosham. At the large roundabout is **Ports Bridge**, across Port's Creek, which separates Portsea Island from the mainland. The huge rampart defending the city from attack has been partly dug away for road-widening. Originally there were two arches through it. Take the next fork left and then the next fork right. Follow on straight ahead (the road signposted 'Fratton and Seafront'). Pass **St Mary's, Portsea**, a large, handsome church dating from 1889, on the left. At Fratton Bridge fork right into Victoria Road North and Victoria Road South. Cross Clarendon Road into Lennox Street South and emerge on to Southsea Common, where there are many large car parks.

Walk 1: Southsea. Southsea Castle (1) (see above) is on the sea front. Dating from 1538-44, it consists of a square keep, set within a courtyard surrounded by a curtain wall protected by a dry moat. It was remodelled by Sir Bernard de Gomme, who placed the royal arms of Charles II over the gateway. The castle now houses an interesting museum, illustrating Portsmouth's history as a port and garrison. Another museum, of natural history, is in **Cumberland House,** St Helen's Parade, near the Canoe Lake.

From the castle it is best to drive again, westward along the front. Just before reaching **Clarence Pier**, note the anchor of HMS *Victory*, preserved on the beach. Turn right at Clarence Pier and take Pier Road across the Common. Take the first left into Pembroke Road, in which is **Nelson's statue**, on the right. Turn left into Penny Street, which leads into Grand Parade, a car park.

Walk 2: the old town. Start at the **Square Tower** (2), standing at the bottom of High Street and dating from 1494. On the north face is a bust of Charles I, given by him to the town in 1635, and commemorating his safe return, as Prince of Wales, from a journey to France and Spain in 1623 in search of a wife. It was the work of Hubrecht le Sueur, a famous sculptor born in the Channel Islands. Adjoining the tower is the Sally Port, with the inscription: 'Heroes innumerable have embarked to fight their country's battles.' This was the principal landing place for important visitors. Katharine of Braganza landed there on 14th May 1662, before her marriage to Charles II at the Domus Dei (see below). Beyond this is the **Round Tower** (3), dating from the early fifteenth century. From here to Gosport, on the opposite shore, was stretched a huge chain, held taut by capstans. It was described by Leland as a 'mightie chaine of yron', and cost £40. Return to the Square Tower and go eastwards along the sea-wall. On the left is

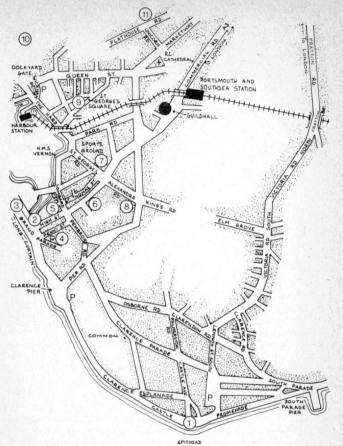

PORTSMOUTH

1. Southsea Castle
2. Square Tower
3. Round Tower
4. Garrison Church
5. Cathedral
6. Buckingham House

7. Landport Gate
8. City Museum and Art Gallery
9. St George's Church
10. HMS Victory
11. Unicorn Gate

the **Long Curtain**, the last remaining portion of de Gomme's defences (see above). Return to the Square Tower again, and go by Grand Parade and Governor's Green to the **Garrison Church** (4). This was originally the Domus Dei, a religious foundation of Peter de Rupibus, Bishop of Winchester, c. 1212, to care for the sick and needy. Suppressed at the Dissolution in 1540, the old hospital building later became the Governor's residence. In Victorian times only the chapel remained, and this was restored in 1867-8 and became the Garrison Church. During the Second World War the nave was severely damaged and has never been repaired, but services are still held in the chancel.

Now proceed along the High Street to the **Cathedral of St Thomas of Canterbury** (5). This building shows many different kinds of architecture. The chancel is part of the original church on this site and is good Early English work of c. 1190-1200, the transepts being rather later. The nave and tower were rebuilt in the Classical style after the church had been damaged during the Civil War. The tower is surmounted by a dome and above this is a cupola. The weather-vane (1710) was blown down and is preserved in the church; a new weather-vane, seven feet long, is on the tower. The new nave, to the design of Sir Charles Nicholson, was begun in 1938, but work upon it stopped the next year, when only three bays in the Gothic style had been completed. It is proposed to complete the building in a modernistic style. The Navy Aisle, commemorating much naval history, was added by Sir Charles Nicholson. The stained glass of the cathedral commemorates various people prominent in Portsmouth's history. The most notable monument is that of the Duke of Buckingham, believed to be the work of Nicholas Stone, a well-known sculptor of his day.

The house where Buckingham was murdered is further along High Street, on the opposite side (6). It carries a plaque, and is now known as **Buckingham House**, but was called Spotted Dog House at the time of the murder.

To the north of the cathedral are **Lombard Street** and **St Thomas Street** in which are seventeenth-century houses, some with Dutch gables. At the far end of the street on the north side of St George's Road is the **Landport Gate**, the last surviving gateway of old Portsmouth (7). It dates from 1760 and may have been designed by Nicholas Hawksmoor, designer of the towers of Westminster Abbey. It now leads only to a sports ground. A short distance down Alexandra Road (on the other side of High Street roundabout) is the **City Museum and Art Gallery** (8).

Walk 3: Portsea. Now return to the car, and drive up High Street and left into St George's Road. Just past the railway is **St George's**

Church (9), a good building of 1754. It was damaged by bombing but has been well restored. Continue along the Hard to the Dockyard Gate. There is a multi-storey car park in Wickham Street.

The **Dockyard** can be visited on foot between 10.30 a.m. and 5.30 p.m. on weekdays, and 1 p.m. and 5 p.m. on Sundays. There are many eighteenth-century buildings. On the left is the **Semaphore Tower**, into the base of which has been built the old Lion Gate, dating from 1788 and formerly one of Portsea's gateways. Beyond, on the right, is **HMS Victory** (10), the flagship of Lord Nelson and now that of the Commander-in-Chief, and the shrine of the Royal Navy (plate 9). Launched at Chatham in 1765, she served for many years before being chosen by Nelson for her good sailing qualities. After the Battle of Trafalgar she rode at anchor in the harbour for more than a century until 1922, when she was moved into No. 2 Dock, on the site of the oldest dry-dock in the world. Opposite the *Victory* is the **Victory Museum** which contains a wonderful panorama of the Battle of Trafalgar by W. L. Wyllie RA, and many other items of naval interest including ships' figureheads and models.

Except for HMS *Victory*, the Museum and **St Ann's Church** the Dockyard is not open to visitors. St Ann's is the parish church of the Dockyard, and dates from 1785-6. After severe bomb damage it was very well restored in 1955-6. The wonderful ceiling was preserved during the course of repairs. Note particularly the royal arms on the west gallery, which may have come from an admiral's barge. The east window depicts 'Christ ascendant over the Dockyard', the Dockyard shown as it appeared after the war (Enquire at gateway).

Return to the car once more and drive along Queen Street, left into Alfred Road, and left again into Unicorn Road. At the top of this is **Unicorn Gate** (11), one of the most handsome of the Dockyard gateways. Here turn right along Flathouse Road, and by the Royal Portsmouth Hospital right into Fitzherbert Street, then left into Commercial Road (A3). **No. 293 Commercial Road** is Dickens's birthplace, now a museum (open November to February 10 a.m. to 4 p.m., and March to October 10 a.m. to 6 p.m.). Park in a side street, as Commercial Road is not a possible stopping place. Charles Dickens was born there in 1812 while his father was employed at the Dockyard, but the family soon moved to London.

From here one can drive back northwards to Cosham, and westwards into Southampton Road for **Portchester Castle** (see above).

Ringwood

History. Known from Roman times, Ringwood is a thriving market town on the Avon, west of the New Forest. It is noted for fresh-water fishing, and has some light industries. In 1685 the Duke of Monmouth was lodged in West Street after his defeat at Sedgemoor. From his lodging (now called Monmouth House), he wrote to his uncle James II begging for mercy, but this was refused, and Monmouth was later beheaded on Tower Hill.

Approach. Entering Ringwood by the Southampton road (A31), turn left off the bypass at signs for the town centre. Continue down Southampton Road. Off the second turn right is the **Manor House** (1737) (1). The third turn right, Meeting House Lane, leads into a large car park on the right.

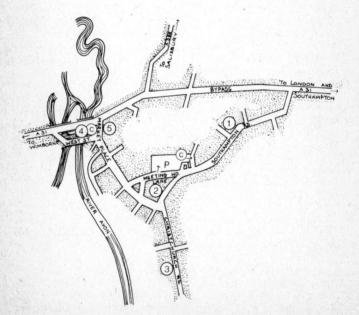

RINGWOOD

1. Manor House
2. Unitarian chapel
3. Netherbrook Gallery

4. Monmouth House
5. Church

Walk. Walk westward along Meeting House Lane. On the left is an interesting brick **Unitarian chapel** (1727) with box-pews and galleries (2). Turn left and left again into Christchurch Road. No. 44 on the right (3) is a fine, late eighteenth-century brick house, now **Netherbrook Gallery** antique shop, with two old ships' figureheads in front. Return along Christchurch Road to the Market Place. Several shops retain their Georgian bow-windows, an attractive feature of the town. In West Street, to the left off the Market Place, are **Monmouth House** (4), and pretty old thatched cottages near the river. The **church** (5), on the right just beyond the Market Place, is good Victorian Gothic (1854-5). In the chancel floor is a fine brass to Prebendary John Prophete (d. 1416), Dean of Hereford and later of York, in rich eucharistic vestments.

Romsey

History. Romsey grew up into a town when Edward the Elder, son of Alfred the Great, founded a Saxon nunnery there in 907. Edward's daughter Elfleda was the first abbess. Edgar, grandson of Edward, reconstituted the nunnery as a Benedictine house. It was always closely connected with royalty. King Stephen's daughter Mary became abbess, and her uncle Bishop Henri de Blois of Winchester (1129-71) probably built much of the Norman abbey as we see it today. At the Dissolution the townspeople, who had previously worshipped only in the north aisle of the nave, bought the church for £100. The deed of sale, signed by Henry VIII, is still preserved.

Approach. Enter Romsey from the bypass (A31 from Winchester, A27 from Southampton), turn right into Palmerston Road and left into Broadwater; there is a car park on the right with a footpath through to the Market Place.

Walk. Walk across the Market Place (plate 8), in which is a **statue of Lord Palmerston** (1), to the **Abbey Church** off the north-west corner (2). This magnificent church was begun c. 1125 and carried on westward as far as the third bay of the nave, when the work was interrupted. It was resumed in beautiful Early English style. The apse of the Saxon church, which the Norman building replaced, was discovered in 1900 below the present chancel. There are two other relics of the Saxon church. A small rood, found built into a wall facing inwards, presumably to protect it from the reformers of the sixteenth century, is now a reredos in one of the east chapels. Outside the south door, in what were the nuns' cloisters,

91

is a wonderful early eleventh-century life-sized rood, with the hand of God above it. In the north transept is another treasure, an early sixteenth-century painted wooden reredos depicting the Resurrection of Christ, and a number of figures of saints. The upper part, which showed Christ in Glory, is missing. A Norman capital in the north chancel aisle has a most realistic battle scene. The south transept contains a beautiful, thirteenth-century Purbeck-marble effigy of a lady. Above it is a fourteenth-century canopy. A monument to John St Barbe (1658) and his wife is said to be the work of Thomas Stanton, Master of the Stonemasons' Company. On the right-hand side of the apse in the north aisle is a beautiful memorial by Fuchs (1911) to Maud Ashley, mother of Lady Mountbatten, who was much beloved in Romsey and did much for the town. There are numerous other interesting monuments in the nave.

East of the Abbey, across Church Street in a narrow lane, is **King John's House** (3), a hunting lodge built by John c. 1206, accidentally rediscovered in 1927 by the late Mr W. J. Andrew FSA. Henry III, son of John, gave it to the abbess as a guest-house. After the Dissolution it became a private residence, and in the eighteenth century it was used as a workhouse. It is built of flint, and has windows with dog-tooth ornamentation. A set of shields, roughly scratched on the plaster walls, portrays the arms of some barons and records a state visit to Romsey in 1306

There are several old inns. The **White Horse** (4), on the north side of Market Place, is of Tudor date with Georgian front. It has much old timber-work, and in the bar and lounge some wall paintings. The **Tudor Rose** (5), on the south side of Market Place, has a sixteenth-century timber-framed room with a stone fireplace on the first floor. The **Dolphin** (6) has a pleasant bow-windowed front. The **Bishop Blaise**, in Winchester Street (7), recalls Romsey's association with the wool trade, Blaise being the patron saint of woolcombers. The former **Swan** inn (8), in the Market Place, is a much-restored house retaining the iron bracket from which the sign hung. A soldier, who committed murder during the Civil War, was hanged from this bracket.

South of the bypass is **Broadlands Park**, where Lord Palmerston lived. It is now the seat of Lord Louis Mountbatten. Queen Elizabeth II spent part of her honeymoon there.

In the neighbourhood. Mottisfont Abbey four miles north-west along A3056, was an Augustinian priory founded in the twelfth century and converted into a mansion by Lord Chancellor Sandys after the Dissolution. The drawing-room contains *trompe l'oeil* paintings in the Gothick manner by Rex Whistler. Mrs Russell

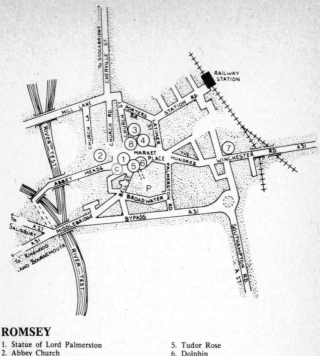

ROMSEY

1. Statue of Lord Palmerston
2. Abbey Church
3. King John's House
4. White Horse

5. Tudor Rose
6. Dolphin
7. Bishop Blaise
8. Swan

gave the abbey to the National Trust in 1957. The Whistler Room and Cellarium are open April to September, Wednesdays and Saturdays, 2.30 p.m. to 6 p.m.

Southampton

History. There were settlements at Southampton from Neolithic times onwards. The Romans established a fort, *Clausentum* (now Bitterne), in a loop of the Itchen. Early Saxon settlements included

Hamwih and Hamtun, and the name *Suthamptune* appears in a charter of King Edgar in the tenth century. Canute of Denmark was chosen king at Southampton in 1017, and the site of his legendary rebuke to his courtiers who asked him to turn back the tide is the Canute Inn in Canute Road. The Normans built a town in the peninsula between the Itchen and Test, with an earthen bank and ditch across the neck of the peninsula, with a stone gateway, now incorporated in the Bargate (see below).

The town was frequently raided by the French and in the worst raid, in 1338, was completely sacked and burned. After this walls were built along the south and west sides of the town, previously thought to have been sufficiently defended by the water.

In 1415 three conspirators against Henry V, the Earl of Cambridge, Lord Scrope of Masham and Sir Thomas Grey of Northumberland, were executed at the Bargate. After this Henry's troops embarked for France and the Battle of Agincourt. The town was always a centre of trade, first mainly of wine, and later of wool exports and imports of more exotic goods from the Mediterranean and the East.

Queen Elizabeth I paid a visit in 1591 and was welcomed at the north front of the Bargate by the Mayor and Corporation and presented with a purse of £40. Charles II, similarly welcomed in 1669, received 150 guineas. The Pilgrim Fathers sailed from Southampton for the New World in the *Mayflower* in 1620. In the eighteenth century the town became a fashionable spa.

Dock facilities for both passengers and goods have expanded rapidly. In the Second World War the town suffered very severely from air raids, but has since been largely restored.

Approach. Approaching Southampton from the north by the A33, follow signposts 'Inner Ring Road and Town Centre'. Where East Park on the right comes to an end and the shopping area starts, there is a small roundabout with an island on which is a handsome **gas lamp column** (1), commemorating the first lighting of the town by gas. Keep straight on from the roundabout and shortly cross East Street. A few yards beyond this, on the right, a small road leads to a multi-storey car park, convenient for the centre of the city.

Walk. On emerging from the car park, follow the street named Back of the Walls, where part of the town wall remains, to East Street. Here turn left and, shortly, right into York Buildings. This leads to a modern gap cut through the town wall. Turn right here for the **Polymond Tower** (2) at the north-east angle of the town defences. Turn back from here, past two turrets and up some steps, through an arcade of shops and so to the **Bargate** (3). This

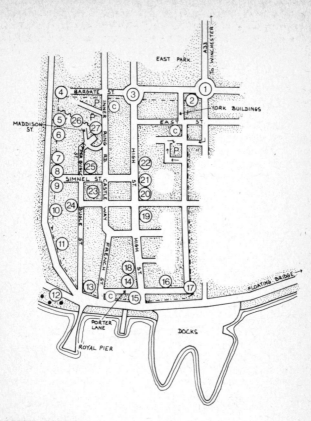

SOUTHAMPTON

1. Gas lamp column
2. Polymond Tower
3. Bargate
4. Arundel Tower
5. Catchcold Tower
6. Forty Steps
7. Vaults
8. Water Gate of the castle
9. The Arcades
10. Norman House
11. Westgate
12. Mayflower Monument
13. Wool House
14. 'Canute's Palace'
15. Water Gate
16. St Julian's and God's House
17. Gateway by God's House Tower
18. Quilter's Vault
19. Red Lion inn
20. Ruins of Holy Rood church
21. Dolphin hotel
22. Star hotel
23. St Michael's church
24. Tudor House Museum
25. Vaulted cellar
26. Bailey wall of castle
27. Castle gate

fine gate, which now houses a museum, was the north gate of the old walled town. There is now a road all round it, but the remains of the old walls can be seen on either side. The original Norman arch is inside the Bargate, and a pair of drum towers was added in the thirteenth century, the south front facing down the High Street in the fourteenth century, and a three-sided fore-building in the fifteenth century. On the south front is a statue of George III dressed as a Roman emperor. Proceeding westward from the Bargate, cross the Inner Ring Road by a subway, and descend the hill to the thirteenth-century drum-tower, **Arundel Tower** (4), the north-west corner of the city's defences. Turn left along Western Esplanade, reclaimed from where the Test formerly lapped the walls. A few yards southward is the fifteenth-century **Catchcold Tower** (5), which has three gunports. Beyond it are the **Forty Steps** (1853) (6) giving access to the ramparts.

South of the steps, the fourteenth-century town wall is replaced by the castle wall, with twelfth-century buttresses. (See more about the castle below.) In this section of the wall are two **vaults** (7), formerly used for the king's wine and other stores. In a recess just south of the vaults is the fourteenth-century **Water Gate** (8) of the castle, now blocked, but formerly giving access from the castle above to a private quay belonging to the king. A little further on is the most interesting part of the walls, the sentries' walk on top of it being carried on **The Arcades** (9), arches built into the fronts of the original houses standing here when the circuit of the walls was completed after the French raid of 1338 (plate 12). Beyond the arch of the Blue Anchor Postern Gate is the **Norman House** (10), dating from about 1150-75, one of the oldest examples of domestic architecture in England. The upper windows are original, but the lower ones were blocked and pierced in c. 1360 with gunports, which must be some of the earliest in existence (see also below).

Next comes the fourteenth-century **Westgate** (11), through which troops marched on to the quay on their way to Crecy in 1346 and Agincourt in 1415. Adjoining the Westgate on the inner side of the wall is the so-called **Guard Room**, more probably really a merchant's store, an early Tudor timbered building on a stone base. It has a fine chestnut roof. Turn back through the Westgate and continue the walk with the wall, now more fragmentary, on your left. Near here are the **Mayflower Monument** (12), with a model of the Pilgrim Fathers' ship on a pillar of Portland stone, and a **memorial fountain** to Mary Ann Rogers, the stewardess who sacrificed her life by giving up her life-belt to a passenger in the wreck of the *Stella* off the Channel Islands in 1899.

A little further on is the **Wool House** (13), a fourteenth-century warehouse, with heavy cylindrical buttresses and a fine roof of Spanish chestnut. The wool trade, especially with Flanders, flourished until Henry VIII restricted wool export and the whole trade of Southampton declined. In the Napoleonic Wars, French prisoners were lodged in the Wool House, and some carved their names on the roof beams. The Wool House is now an excellent maritime museum.

Next cross French Street, where the Norman inhabitants lived after the Conquest. A large red-brick warehouse stands on the quay, and behind it is Porters Lane, in which is the ruin of a Norman house known as **Canute's Palace** (14), but wrongly, as it was built more than a century after his reign.

At the south end of the High Street (formerly English Street), now reached, stands what is left of the **Water Gate** (15). The footings of the western side of the gateway still remain and the western tower has been well restored by the corporation. Cross the High Street and enter Winkle Street. **St Julian's and God's House** (16) was founded as an almshouse for the aged poor by Gervase le Riche in 1185. Part of the Norman work remains, though the building and chapel were much rebuilt in the nineteenth century. Now pass through a fourteenth-century gateway (17) and **God's House Tower** is on your left. Built in the fifteenth century, it was an important spur-work at the south-east angle of the town walls. A turret can be seen in the narrow street known as Back of the Walls. The tower was the headquarters of the town gunner, who was paid sixpence a day, a salary then exceeding that of the town clerk. Guns fired from this tower caused a French fleet to retreat in 1457. The tower also protected the sluices controlling the flow of water into the town ditch. Traces of the blocked archway over it are visible at the base of the tower. From 1775 until 1855 the tower was used as the town gaol. Later it has been excellently restored by the corporation and is now a most interesting museum of archaeology.

Return to the High Street and walk northwards. On the left is a medieval cellar, **Quilter's Vault** (18). Inside the **Red Lion** inn, on the right, is a perfectly preserved medieval hall known as the Court Room (19). The trial of the conspirators against Henry V, mentioned above, probably took place here.

Further north are the ruins of **Holy Rood church** (20), largely destroyed in an air raid in 1940. It has been preserved as a memorial garden to the Merchant Navy, and the tower, with its clock with quarter-jack figures, has been restored, though the spire went in the raid. The **Dolphin** hotel (21), a little further north, has Georgian bow-windows said to be the largest in England. It was a great social centre when Southampton was a fashionable spa, and Jane Austen often danced there. The original coach archway into the yard remains. The **Star** hotel (22), a little higher up the street, also retains its coach archway, with a notice on it advertising a coach to London.

Return to Holy Rood church and turn right for **St Michael's church** (23). This has Norman crossing arches under the tower, a Norman font of Tournai marble (one of only seven in England, four being in Hampshire) and two medieval brass lecterns, one fourteenth century from Holy Rood, and the other fifteenth-century. The spire is maintained by Trinity House as a seamark. Opposite the west end of the church is the **Tudor House** now a museum (24), built by Sir John Dawtrey of Petworth, and later occupied by Sir Richard Lyster, Chief Baron of the Exchequer and Lord Chief Justice (1546-52). The fine banqueting hall has a minstrels' gallery. At the back of the house is a garden leading to the Norman house (see above). A Norman chimney, revealed after an air raid in another part of the town, has been built into the ruins.

From Tudor House, walk northward along Bugle Street, passing an old **vaulted cellar** (25) at the corner of Simnel Street. Off Upper Bugle Street is the site of the **castle**, which was royal property and was used by visiting monarchs until after the reign of Elizabeth I. A block of modern flats now stands on the site of the keep. A little beyond the Juniper Berry inn on the left, a short road, Maddison Street, leads to the **bailey wall** of the castle, built upon a series of arches (26). Most of these are filled in, but one is open. Walk through this into a car park, and a few yards to the right, beside Castle Way (Inner Ring Road) are the remains of the **castle gate** (27). Walk up Castle Way, and right into Bargate Street to return to the Bargate.

In the neighbourhood. Netley Abbey, south-east of Southampton, was a Cistercian monastery, colonised from the mother-house of Beaulieu Abbey by Henry III in 1239. At the Dissolution, the ruins were converted into a house by the Marquess of Winchester, but hardly anything of this remains. A Southampton builder named Taylor later bought the abbey ruins, intending to demolish them, but the tracery of the great west window fell on him and killed him. This was considered a judgement of God, and the rest of the beautiful ruins were spared. They are now kept by the Department of the Environment.

To reach Netley Abbey from Southampton, cross the river Itchen by the Floating Bridge, take the third turn right, Victoria Road, then turn left into Weston Grove Road and follow this on into Archery Road, Weston Parade and Abbey Hill.

Whitchurch

History. This small town returned two members to Parliament from the time of Elizabeth I until 1832. In coaching days it was a very busy road junction, and the White Hart hotel dates from that period.

Approach from Basingstoke by B3400 and crossing the A34 Winchester-Newbury road, bear right into Bell Street; the car park is on the left.

Walk. Return down Bell Street to the crossroads. On the left is the Georgian **Town Hall** (1), with cupola. Opposite is the picturesque **White Hart** (2). This had at one time a room called 'The Commandment Room'. Nobody knew why, but during some alterations an oil painting, depicting the Commandments and punishments for breaking them, was discovered hidden in a wall. Dating from 1612, it was probably hidden during the Commonwealth. The inn gave it back to the church. The **church**, in Church Street (3), was drastically restored in 1868, but retains a few old features, including a fifteenth-century font, the Commandments picture, and, most remarkable, a headstone to an Anglo-Saxon lady, Frith-

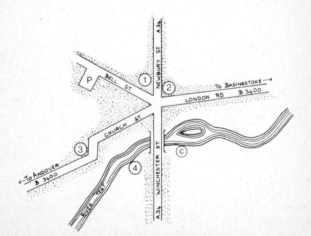

WHITCHURCH

1. Town Hall
2. White Hart

3. Church
4. Silk mill

burga, with a still legible inscription, and a bust of Christ sculptured in relief. Off Winchester Street to the right, is a Georgian **silk mill** on the river Test (4).

Winchester

History. In prehistoric times there was probably a settlement by the ford over the river Itchen, and in the Iron Age a great camp was built on St Catherine's Hill on the east bank of the river. Later the Romans established their *Venta Belgarum* on the west bank. In Saxon times Winchester was the capital of Wessex. After the conversion of King Cynegils to Christianity by St Birinus of Dorchester (Oxfordshire), the first cathedral was built at Winchester. The city was capital of all England from the reign of Egbert (827) until the thirteenth century. A new minster was built north of the Saxon one by Edward the Elder, son of King Alfred. Recent excavation has revealed much of these old minsters. Alfred (870-901) made Winchester his headquarters in his fight against the Danes, and St Swithun, his tutor (patron saint and Bishop 852-62), also defended the city against the Danes, and fortified the Close.

William the Conqueror was crowned in Winchester as well as in London. In medieval times it was an important trading centre and wool staple town. After the Plague of 1666 it diminished in importance, but in the eighteenth and nineteenth centuries grew to its present position as county town, cathedral city and educational and military centre.

Approach. Entering Winchester down Magdalen Hill (A31) and by the bridge over the Itchen, turn right into Eastgate Street, and left into Friarsgate. This leads via Lower Brook Street into Middle Brook Street where there is a large car park.

Walk. From the car park, take any south-running road into High Street, where turn right. The middle part of High Street is a pedestrian precinct. On the south side of the street there is a row of colonnaded shops, some new and some medieval, called the Pentice. Just above this is the beautiful fifteenth-century **Butter Cross** (1), restored in Victorian times, but with one original statue, of St John the Evangelist, on the south side. Adjoining the Cross is a fourteenth-century timber-framed house, now a cafe. Further up on the left is the former Guildhall (now **Lloyds Bank**) with a handsome clock overhanging the street, and a statue of Queen Anne on the facade (2). It dates from 1713. Opposite is the fifteenth-century **God Begot House** (3), with a modern reproduction

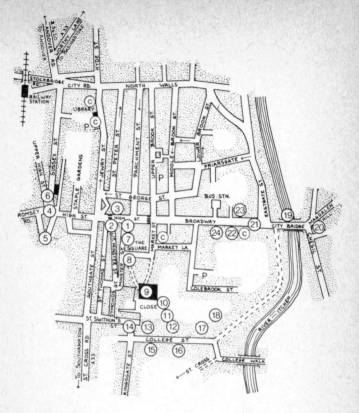

WINCHESTER

1. Butter Cross
2. Lloyds Bank
3. God Begot House
4. Westgate
5. Castle
6. Plague Monument
7. St Lawrence's church
8. City Museum
9. Cathedral
10. Chapter house
11. Deanery
12. Pilgrims' School

13. Cheyney Court
14. King's Gate
15. Jane Austen's house
16. College of St Mary
17. Wolvesey Palace
18. Wolvesey Castle
19. City Mill
20. Old Chesil Rectory
21. King Alfred's statue
22. Abbey House
23. St John's Hospital
24. Guildhall

front, but with the original side in Royal Oak Passage. **Searl's House**, a fine brick mansion of seventeenth-century date in Southgate Street, now houses the Royal Hampshire Regiment Museum. At the top of High Street is the **Westgate** (plate 11), the only survivor of the major city gates (4). It is mainly thirteenth-century, but the west face is fourteenth-century and has two early gunports. Over the gate is a museum (admission free) which includes the standard weights and measures as fixed in Tudor times. From the roof there is a fine view over the city, with St Giles' Hill to the east and St Catherine's Hill to the south-east. South of the Westgate stood the **castle** (5), mainly destroyed by Cromwell during the Civil War. Its fine early thirteenth-century Great Hall remains, the arcades of which are of Purbeck marble. On the west wall hangs the so-called 'King Arthur's Round Table', now supposed to be thirteenth-century, and repainted in Tudor times. The royal palace adjoined the hall at this end: Henry III was the last king to be born there. The site of the massive keep of the castle was discovered by excavation in 1968. North of the Westgate is the **Plague Monument** (6), where country folk used to deposit their goods for the plague-stricken city, and the citizens deposited their money in a bowl of vinegar.

Return down High Street to the Butter Cross, and turn right through a little passage into the Square. In the passage is a Norman pillar, sole relic of William the Conqueror's palace, which was destroyed by fire during the civil war between Stephen and Matilda. The little fifteenth-century **church of St Lawrence**, on the left, is believed to occupy the site of the chapel of the Norman palace (7).

In the Square is the **City Museum** (8), with interesting collections of local finds. From the museum, walk through the avenue of limes to the **cathedral** (9) (plate 10). In the south-west corner of the cathedral churchyard is the tomb, with amusing epitaph, of Colonel Thomas Thetcher, who 'caught his death by drinking cold small beer'.

The earliest parts of the present cathedral are the plain Norman transepts, built by Bishop Walkelyn. The tower, later and richer in style, was rebuilt after a former one had fallen. The Norman choir was extended eastward by Bishop de Lucy (1189-1204), who also built the Early English work east of the great screen and the first bay of the Lady Chapel. The remodelled Norman apse, and the old choir as it is now, date from about 1330. The crypt shows the plan of the original Norman apse. Bishop Edington demolished the two west towers and is said to be responsible for the present west front. William of Wykeham, Bishop from 1367 to 1404 and Chancellor to Edward III and Richard II, rebuilt the magnificent nave in

Perpendicular style. The great screen is early fifteenth-century, though the figures are modern restorations. Bishop Fox added the side screen and remodelled the choir aisles. The Lady Chapel at the east end was added in the Perpendicular style.

Among the many treasures of the Cathedral are the twelfth-century Norman font of Tournai marble, carved with legends of St Nicholas of Myra; the chantry chapels of William of Wykeham and other famous bishops; a Purbeck-marble tomb believed to be that of William Rufus; carved choir stalls and misereres; Prior Silkstede's richly carved pulpit; Renaissance mortuary chests on top of the side-screens, alleged to contain the bones of Cynegils, Canute and other kings; wall-paintings in the Lady Chapel; the chair used by Queen Mary Tudor when she married Philip of Spain; and the graves of Izaac Walton (1683), author of *The Compleat Angler*, and Jane Austen (1817).

The shrine of St Swithun, a great resort of pilgrims, was unfortunately destroyed at the Reformation. The cathedral is open to the public except at times of divine service.

From the cathedral a narrow passage by the south-west corner leads into the Close, where the former monastery stood. It contains some beautiful old houses, the Norman arcade of the former **chapter house** (10), the thirteenth-century **Deanery** (11), originally the prior's hall of the monastery, the seventeenth-century **Pilgrims School** (12) with the thirteenth-century Pilgrims Hall at its north end with a fine hammer-beam roof, and stables used by pilgrims on their way from Winchester to Canterbury, and the fifteenth-century three-gabled **Cheyney Court** (13), where bishops formerly held their courts for governing this part of the city.

By Cheyney Court is a gate into St Swithun's Street, which has the Close wall on the right, and remains of the old city wall behind houses on the left. Here there was a battle between the rebel Simon de Montfort and the forces of Henry III. Turn left under **King's Gate** (14), above which is the tiny church of St Swithun-upon-Kingsgate. Turn left into College Street. A tablet, on the right, marks the house where Jane Austen died (15), and a little beyond is the **College of St Mary** (16), founded by William of Wykeham in 1382 for 'seventy poor and needy scholars', and now one of our most famous schools. The College is open weekdays from 10 a.m. to 6 p.m. and on Sundays from 2 p.m. to 6 p.m., but visitors must be conducted round by guides. There are beautiful statues of the Virgin and Child over the gateways of the outer and inner courts. There are two original quadrangles; a chapel, much restored but containing some old misere seats and a fan-tracery wooden roof; a dining hall with fine oak roof and the famous allegorical painting of the 'Trusty Servant' at the entrance to the kitchen;

cloisters with good stone roof; and the 'School Room' designed by Wren (1687), with bronze statue of the founder, by Cibber. (The War Memorial Cloisters are entered from Kingsgate Street).

On the left of College Street is **Wolvesey Palace** (17), residence of the Bishop. A small gateway near the palace leads to the bishop's fence, a public right of way to Wolvesey Castle. The original castle was built by Bishop de Blois in the early twelfth century, but was ruined by Cromwell in the Civil War. The keep and great hall are recognisable, and more is being discovered by excavation.

A little further along College Street turn right into College Walk. From this a delightful footpath follows a stream through the Meads to **St Cross Hospital**. (This is otherwise reached by road along Southgate Street and St Cross Road; frequent buses from the bus station in Broadway.) This beautiful medieval almshouse was founded by Bishop Henri de Blois, brother of King Stephen, in 1133 for thirteen poor brethren, who wore black gowns with a silver cross, as their successors do to this day. In 1455 Cardinal Beaufort added an 'Almshouse of Noble Poverty' to the foundation; these brethren wear a purple gown. A dole of bread and beer is still given to any traveller who asks for it at the porter's lodge, until the daily supply is exhausted. St Cross is open to the public daily. It has a fifteenth-century inner gatehouse, a dining hall and interesting old kitchen on the north side of the quadrangle, the brethren's houses on the west, and an ambulatory on the east with seventeenth-century gallery. The beautiful church has Transitional Norman choir and transepts, thirteenth-century nave, fourteenth-century tower, Norman font and other interesting features.

Return to College Street and walk north-eastward along the outside of the city wall, here partly standing to its full height. The path continues by the river Itchen and is here called The Weirs. It leads to the **City Bridge**, an eighteenth-century structure taking the place of one built by St Swithun in Saxon times. Above the bridge is the charming old **City Mill**, now a youth hostel (19). It belonged to the abbess of Wherwell before the Dissolution, then became crown property, and was presented to the citizens of Winchester by Mary Tudor after her wedding festivities. Turn right over the bridge into Chesil Street. The fifteenth-century **Old Chesil Rectory** (20), now a restaurant, is supposed to be the oldest house in Winchester. Return across the bridge to the Broadway, where there is a fine millennary **statue of King Alfred**, by Hamo Thorneycroft (1910) (21). On the left are the Abbey Grounds, on the site of St Mary's Abbey, and the eighteenth-century **Abbey House** (22), the mayoral residence. Opposite is the thirteenth-century chapel of **St John's Hospital** (23), an almshouse founded by Alderman John Devenishe in 1275.

The **Guildhall**, on the left, with clock-tower, is a Victorian building of 1871-3 (24). Return to the car park by walking on up the Broadway and turning right into Middle Brook Street.

Bradford-on-Avon

History. Bradford-on-Avon is one of the most beautiful towns in England, both scenically and architecturally. On the north side of the Avon, across which in old times was the 'broad ford', rise terraces of houses of grey Cotswold stone, the highest terrace being some 200 feet high. It was from this point that Canon Jones, a Victorian vicar, noticed, at the bottom of the hill, a building, which he could not place, with a very high roof, and surrounded by other buildings. Going down to it, he discovered that it was undoubtedly a Saxon church. Full of enthusiasm, he bought the cottage property all round and cleared it away. He then realised that the little church, forgotten through many centuries, was none other than that church of a small monastery founded here by St Aldhelm in 705 and described by William of Malmesbury, the monkish chronicler, as an *ecclesiola* or small church. This wonderful little building (plate 13) consists of a nave, two porches (one lost) and a very small chancel, the chancel arch being only 3 feet 6 inches wide. Expert ecclesiologists have dated the ground stage of the building as Aldhelm's work, but consider that the upper portion is later, probably tenth century.

In 1001 King Ethelred gave the manor of Bradford-on-Avon to the Abbess of Shaftesbury nunnery as a refuge from Danish invaders, but they ravaged the whole district, and Aldhelm's monastery perished in the general holocaust.

All through the medieval period Bradford prospered on its wool trade. In 1265 two representatives of the town were summoned to Parliament. Edward III reorganised the wool trade in 1331, making Bristol a staple (or market) town for wool instead of exporting the raw material to Flanders for manufacture. Thus began the long association of Bradford with cloth-making. The antiquary Leland visited Bradford in 1540 and noted that 'Al the town of Bradford standith by clooth making.' In 1659 Paul Methuen, a prominent clothier, introduced a fine kind of weaving from abroad and brought over some clothiers from Holland to teach the new methods. These first settlers lived in a quarter known as Dutch Barton, where some of their cottages are still standing. By the end of the seventeenth century many cottages fitted with looms were built, all with wide windows back and front, enabling the weavers to work from dawn until dusk. Records show that in 1723 there were twenty-five master clothiers in the town. During the eighteenth century machinery and the factory system began to be introduced, accompanied by a certain amount of

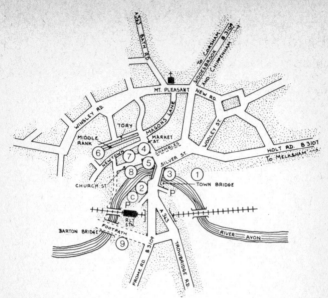

BRADFORD-ON-AVON

1. The Hall
2. Westbury House
3. Blind House
4. Roman Catholic church
5. Swan hotel

6. Chapel of St Mary
7. Church House
8. Rubber factory
9. Barton Farm

rioting and bloodshed.

The clothing industry continued to prosper until c. 1840, but after that a depression, caused partly by the failure of a local bank, began, and some mills were closed and their workers migrated to other districts. The last clothing mill closed in 1905, but by that time the rubber industry had been introduced and is still flourishing, some of the clothing mills having been converted to rubber factories.

During the seventeenth and eighteenth centuries, many fine houses were built by the wool merchants, the finest being **The Hall** (1), built early in the seventeenth century by John Hall, one of a family long connected with the clothing trade. (The house is not open to the public, but the grounds may sometimes be viewed by special permission.)

Approach Bradford by A363 from Trowbridge, and there are car parks just short of the Avon bridge, one on the left behind **Westbury House** council offices (2), and one on the right adjoining the bridge.

Walk 1: to the Tory. Start from the **Town Bridge**, two arches of which are medieval, being ribbed and pointed; the others are eighteenth-century. On the bridge is the **'Blind House'** or lock-up (3), probably once a chapel. There are only three other bridge-chapels in England. At the north end of the bridge, fork right into **Silver Street**. In this, and **Woolley Street** leading left from it, there are some fine Georgian houses. Return along Silver Street and through the **Shambles**, a pedestrian passage containing some old timber-framed shops, into Market Street. On the corner of Market Street and Church Street is the former town hall (1855), now used as a **Roman Catholic church** (4). Opposite this is the **Swan** hotel with pleasant late Georgian facade (5). Walk up the steep hill of Market Street and turn left at the top into the street named **Newtown**. Here are some late seventeenth-century cottages. A steep lane leads up to **Middle Rank**, in which is another row of gabled houses of the late seventeenth century, and the **Sion Baptist Church**, c. 1698. Above this again is the top tier of terrace houses, known as **Tory**, a Saxon word for hill, with no political associations. Along this runs a footpath. The houses at the west end of the terrace (nos. 27-32) are late Georgian; the remainder rather earlier. The view from here is superb and very extensive. Below are the huddled roofs of the old town, and in the distance on the horizon are the Westbury White Horse and Cley Hill, a commanding height near Warminster. At the west end of the terrace is the **Chapel of St Mary** (6), adjoining a house formerly used as a hospice for travellers. Once in ruins, it was restored in 1877. From this point descend to Newtown and so back to the town.

Walk 2. From Town Bridge fork left into Market Street and turn left into Church Street. On the right is the **Church House** (7), built by Thomas Horton, a wealthy clothier who died in 1530. On the left is the imposing **rubber factory** (8), formerly a clothing mill, built in 1875. Next on the right is **Dutch Barton** (seventeenth-century; see above) and up a short ascent on the right **Druce's Hill House**, fine Georgian, formerly the home of the Druce family, Quaker clothiers. **Abbey House**, facing west, is late eighteenth-century, and beyond that are the **Saxon church** (see above), right, and **Holy Trinity parish church**, left. The latter, originally Norman, has been much enlarged since, and contains many very interesting tombs, including a fine standing monument to Anthony Methuen (1737) by Rysbrack. Beyond the churches, the path climbs to **Barton Orchard**, an eighteenth-century terrace of weavers' houses. This path leads down to a level crossing over the railway, and over the fourteenth-century **Barton Bridge**. Just beyond is **Barton Farm** (9), and here is the magnificent **tithe barn**, 168 feet long. It has two cart entrances and a very fine timber roof. Return to the town by Frome Road and St Margaret's Street. **Westbury House** (see above) was the seat of the Westbury family, and is fine early Georgian. Near it are the car parks.

CALNE

1. Town Hall
2. Lansdowne Arms hotel
3. Bacon factory
4. St Mary's church
5. The Green
6. White Hart hotel

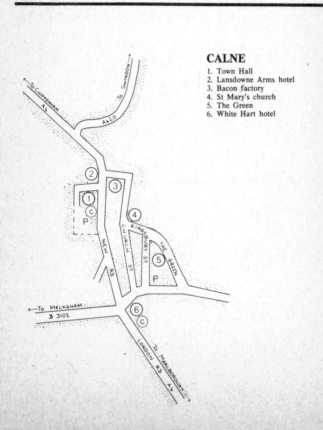

Calne

History. Calne is a pleasant, stone-built town, formerly a cloth town, but now more noted for Wiltshire bacon. A comic incident from pre-Norman times is noted there. A witan met to discuss the celibacy of the clergy. Part of the floor collapsed and the anti-celibates fell through; the celibates, led by St Dunstan, took this as a proof of their own rightness.

Two famous thirteenth-century vicars of Calne were Robert Grostete, afterwards Bishop of Lincoln, and Edmund Rich of Abingdon, later Archbishop of Canterbury, who was canonised.

Approach by the A4 from Marlborough, and drive down New Road; on the left at the bottom are the **Town Hall** (1) and a large car park.

Walk: North of the Town Hall is the late Georgian **Lansdowne Arms** hotel (2). Opposite is the **bacon factory** (3); past this, turn right into Church Street. The **church**, St Mary (4), is mainly Perpendicular outside, but has fine Transition arcades in the nave. The crossing and chancel in Classic style and the late Perpendicular tower were built after the central tower fell in 1638. There are some good houses in Church Street, and above, round **The Green** (5) are many handsome Georgian houses built for prosperous cloth-merchants (plate 15). At the corner of The Green and London Road (A4) is the **White Hart** hotel (6), c. 1800, with columned porch.

Chippenham

History. This attractive, busy, stone-built town dates from Saxon times. King Alfred conducted some of his campaigns against the Danes from there. The town remained a royal estate for many years. It was represented in Parliament in Edward I's time. A charter was granted by Mary I in 1554. At one time mainly devoted to the cloth industry, Chippenham is now a centre for dairying industries, engineering and many others.

Approach by the A4 London road from the south-east, turn right into The Butts just after passing the hospital, go ahead into St Mary Street and from that into Emery Lane car park.

Walk. Return to St Mary's Street, where there are some of the most beautiful houses in Chippenham, including **The Grove** (1) with the remains of a seventeenth-century spa pavilion in its garden. From St Mary's Street turn off to **St Andrew's church** (2), on the south-east corner of the Market Place. The lower part is

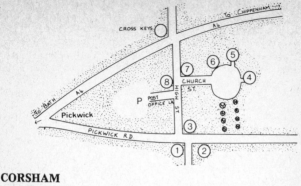

CORSHAM

1. The Grove
2. Hungerford Almshouses
3. Methuen Arms
4. Church

5. Corsham Court
6. Folly
7. Flemish Cottages
8. Town Hall

Walk. Walking south down High Street, one passes many beautiful houses. Across the street at the south end is **The Grove** (1737) (1) and east of this the **Hungerford Almshouses** (2), L-shaped, built by Dame Margaret Hungerford in 1688. Turn back into High Street. On the right is the **Methuen Arms** hotel (1805) (3). In Church Street, right from High Street, are more charming houses and cottages. The **church** (4), originally built in Saxon times, is now largely Norman, with interesting later additions, including the Perpendicular Tropenell Chapel, with a fine altar tomb, separated from the north aisle by a beautiful stone screen with fan-vaulted canopy. There are two chained books, one being Foxe's *Book of Martyrs* (1631-2). A tomb in the north of the churchyard commemorates Sarah Jarvis, who died in 1753, aged 107, having recently cut fresh teeth. In the porch 'lyeth the body of Wm. Tasker, gent, who chose rather to be a door-keeper in the house of his God than to dwell in the tents of wickedness'. He died in 1684.

Corsham Court (5) lies north-west of the church. Built by 'Customer' Smyth, it was added to by Capability Brown and Nash, 1760-5, to house a famous collection of pictures made by the Methuens. It is the seat of Lord Methuen and is leased to the Bath Academy of Art. It is open Sundays all the year round, Wednesdays and Thursdays from April to October, daily except Mondays and Fridays from mid-July to mid-September, and during the Bath Festival and on Bank Holidays, from 11 a.m. to 12.30 p.m. and 2 p.m. to 6 p.m. in summer, 4 p.m. in winter. Near the gate is a **folly**, a large sham ruin (6).

Return to High Street. On the right is a row of charming, gabled seventeenth-century cottages known as the **Flemish Cottages** (7). Nearly opposite is the **Town Hall** (1784) (8).

Cricklade

History. Cricklade is a little town on the A419 from Swindon to Cirencester (part of the Roman road from Winchester to Gloucester). It was inhabited in Roman and Saxon times, as relics from both periods have been found, and it was probably fortified in King Alfred's time. Just north of the town a bridge crosses the river Thames, here only a small stream.

Approach from Swindon by Calcutt Street, turn left into High

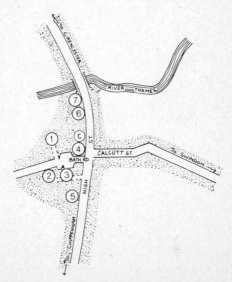

CRICKLADE

1. Fortifications
2. St Samipson's church
3. Robert Jenner's School
4. Vale Hotel
5. House of 1770
6. St Mary's church
7. The Priory

Street and left into Bath Road, where, just by the churchyard, there is a small car park.

Walk. Turn north from here to the town cemetery, where the line of old **fortifications** is marked by a notice (1). Return to the **church** (2), St Sampson's (a Celtic saint). It stands on a ridge, and the glorious pinnacled tower dominates the town and surrounding countryside. The church is of Saxon origin but has been largely rebuilt at various other periods. The tower was probably built by John Dudley, Duke of Northumberland, later beheaded for his conspiracy to put Lady Jane Grey on the throne in 1553. There are many interesting coats of arms in the vaulting of the tower.

From the church return along Bath Road. On the right is **Robert Jenner's School** (3), founded by a London goldsmith in 1651. On the left, facing High Street, is the pleasant old **Vale Hotel** (4). Turn right into High Street, and beyond Bath Road, on the right, is a very fine house dated 1770 (5). There are other good houses on both sides of the street, and at the north end of it, on the left, is the partly Norman **St Mary's church** (6). Beyond this is a group of houses called **The Priory** (7), containing some slight remains, including a blocked arch, of the Hospital of St John the Baptist, a guest-house for poor travellers, founded in the early thirteenth century.

Devizes

History. The name Devizes is thought to come from the Latin *ad Divisas* ('at the boundaries'). Bishop Roger of Salisbury, Chancellor of England, built c. 1109 a castle near the division of his manors of Cannings and Potterne. Queen Matilda occupied the castle for a short time during her fight against Stephen and granted the town a charter in 1141. Many other royalties visited the town and hunted in the district. In the Civil War the Royalists held Devizes after their victory at Roundway Down, but in 1645 Cromwell captured part of the town, and bombarded and practically destroyed the castle. What was left was afterwards pulled down, and rebuilt in the nineteenth century, still in the Norman style. It is now private residences and only the moat and mound and one or two other small relics of the old castle remain. The town is now a large trading centre, especially for goods connected with agriculture.

Approach by the Swindon and London road, A351. Drive along Eastcourt Street and Sidmouth Street and turn right into Monday Market Street. On the left, at the beginning of New Park Street, is a car park.

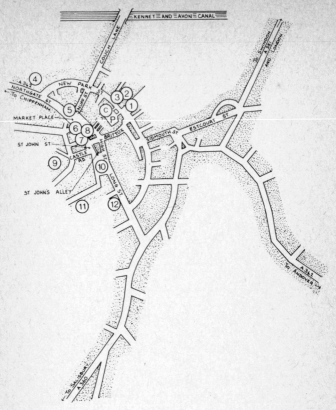

DEVIZES

1. Castle hotel
2. St Mary's church
3. Brownston House
4. Assize Court
5. Black Swan hotel
6. Corn Exchange
7. Bear hotel
8. Market Cross
9. Castle
10. Town Hall
11. St John's church
12. Museum

Walk. Opposite the car park is the handsome, brick **Castle Hotel** (1) and near that is **St Mary's church** (2), partly Norman and partly Perpendicular, much of it rebuilt by William Smyth (died 1436). There is a medieval statue of the Virgin over the Victorian east window. A little further on is the fine **Brownston House** (1720) (3). New Park Road leads out into Northgate Street, where there are some pleasant old houses, some of brick and some of stone. On the right is the **Assize Court** (1835) (4), in Ionic style. From here turn back into the wide Market Place. Interesting buildings here include the **Black Swan** hotel (1737) (5), the **Corn Exchange** (1857) (6) surmounted by a figure of Ceres, the **Bear** hotel (7), mainly eighteenth-century but of much earlier origin, boyhood home of the painter Sir Thomas Lawrence, the **Market Cross** (8), on which is commemorated the death of Ruth Pierce 'by act of God' for dishonesty (plate 19), and the old Classical Town Hall, now business premises, with clock in gable (1750-2). From the Market Place go on into St John Street; Castle Road on the right leads to **Devizes Castle** (9) (see above). Nearly opposite Castle Road, and parallel to St John Street, is St John's Alley, with good fifteenth-century timber-framed houses. The new **Town Hall** (10), by Baldwin of Bath (1806-8), is in Ionic style; in it are some old charters, including one of Henry III (1228). The beautiful **St John's church** (11) is mainly Norman and the work of Bishop Roger. The nave was rebuilt and aisles added in the fifteenth century. The Hungerford and Lamb chapels date from about 1480-5. There is a fifteenth-century oak pulpit, an organ-case thought to be by Grinling Gibbons, and many other treasures. In Long Street, on the right, is the **museum** (12), with an outstanding collection of prehistoric relics (open Tuesday to Saturday inclusive, summer 11 a.m. to 5 p.m., winter 11 a.m. to 4 p.m.). Turn back from the museum up Long Street and High Street, and right into the Brittox, the main street (from the French *breteches*, or outworks of the castle) and left at the end of this back to the car park. The town has many more fine houses, too numerous to mention.

Through the north of the town runs the **Kennet and Avon Canal**, with twenty-nine locks, now unfortunately disused. There are pleasant walks along the towpath.

Roundway Down lies about two miles north (see above).

Malmesbury

History. The great abbey of Malmesbury was founded in Saxon times, during the seventh century, by St Aldhelm. He established a monastery and became the first abbot, holding the office until his death in 709. He was buried in the abbey and his shrine became an object of pilgrimage. King Athelstan, grandson of King Alfred, made many gifts to the abbey and also, in gratitude to the people of Malmesbury for help in fighting the Danes, gave them a five-hundred acre piece of land outside the town, which their descendants still own.

The famous historian, William of Malmesbury, born c. 1090, was a monk here. The first recorded fact about him is that he helped Abbot Gregory to collect a library for the use of the community. He intended to write an account of English history, similar to the works of Bede. He produced two editions of *Gesta Rerum*, the second dedicated to Earl Robert of Gloucester, a patron of literature. William then started to write an account of events since 1127, but the work broke off suddenly in 1142, with an unfulfilled promise that it would be continued. William died c. 1143. He had refused the offer of the abbacy, preferring to continue his literary work. An interesting event recorded by him was the attempted flight of a monk named Elmer. Having equipped himself with wings, he leapt from the top of a tower and glided for about 200 yards, but he then fell and broke both legs, and was a cripple for life.

Malmesbury had a short-lived castle, built by Bishop Roger of Salisbury within the precincts of the abbey, to the horror of the monks. During the Civil War between Stephen and Matilda, the castle was held for the king. After Roger's disgrace and death it was demolished, and there are no traces left. The Normans rebuilt the abbey, probably c. 1160-70. The church, when complete, was 240 feet long and had a central crossing tower, to which was added a tall spire, by repute taller than that of Salisbury. Leland, the sixteenth-century antiquary, described this spire as 'a mighty piramis'. During the fourteenth-century another tower was added, at the west end of the nave. Malmesbury, standing on a hill, surrounded by walls and crowned by this wonderful church, must have been one of England's most beautiful towns at this time.

About 1530 the central tower fell, causing much havoc to both transepts, and some time after Leland's visit the west tower fell, causing more havoc at the west end of the church. In 1539 came the Dissolution of the Monasteries. A rich clothier, William Stumpe, bought the abbey and demolished the choir and Lady Chapel, setting up his looms in some of the monastic buildings. The famous library was wickedly dispersed and lost in the course of these changes. However, though a vandal, Stumpe saved something from the wreck by presenting the nave to the towns-

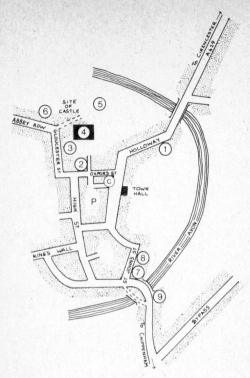

MALMESBURY

1. East Gate
2. Market Cross
3. St Paul's church
4. Church
5. Abbey House
6. Bell hotel
7. St John's Almshouses
8. Court House
9. Textile mill

people for their parish church, and so preserved a fragment of what must have been, when complete, one of the finest monastic churches in Europe.

Approach by the A429 from Cirencester, entering by Holloway; the remains of the **East Gate** of the town may be seen on the left (1). Just after passing Oxford Street on the right there is a car park, also on the right.

Walk. Go into Oxford Street. A little way along it, at the centre of the town, is the **Market Cross** (c. 1500) (2), one of the most magnificent in the country (plate 16). Pass through the Abbey Gate (c. 1800), into the Abbey Churchyard. South-west of the abbey is the tower, with spire, of the former **St Paul's church** (fourteenth century) (3). This now houses the abbey bells and clock. Enter the **church** (4) by the south porch. This magnificent porch is one of the finest in England. The outer arch has eight richly carved orders, three of which are divided into panels with sculptured figures representing biblical scenes. Inside the porch are wall arcades and above, in semicircular panels, are figures of the twelve apostles beneath a flying angel. The inner door has a tympanum showing Christ in glory with an angel on either side.

At the Dissolution the damaged portions of the church were walled off and never repaired. There are now six bays of the original nine. The arcades are late Norman with pointed arches. In the fourteenth century the clerestory was remodelled and the roof vaulted; the pinnacles and flying buttresses were added outside at the same time in order to carry the additional weight of the vaulting. Note the now empty tomb of King Athelstan, with recumbent figure. Note also a curious little projection, rather like a theatre box, in the triforium on the south side. This may possibly have been a watching-chamber for the use of the abbot. The conventual buildings of the monastery surrounded the cloister court, which was on the north side of the church. The reredorter (sanitary conveniences) is now incorporated with the basement of **Abbey House** (5), built by Stumpe to the north-east of the abbey. Incorporated in the **Bell** hotel (6) is some thirteenth-century masonry formerly belonging to the monastic guest-house.

Return to the Market Cross and walk down **High Street**, in which are some good Georgian houses, particularly Nos. 10 and 63, the **King's Arms** hotel with timber-framed back wing, and No. 46 dated 1671, with three gables. To the right off High Street is King's Wall, where part of the town wall formerly stood, and in it is **Athelstan's House**, very handsome, with shell-hood over the doorway. Go on down the High Street. At the bottom of the hill are **St John's Almshouses**, founded in 1694 (7).

Built into them is a Norman arch, a relic of the Hospital of St John of Jerusalem, a Saxon foundation on which Athelstan bestowed £10 a year, which is still paid. Just beyond the almshouses, in St John Street, is the picturesque old **Court House** with its original furniture (8). Matters connected with Athelstan's gift of land are still settled here. Turn back and cross the bridge on the Chippenham road. On the left is a large eighteenth-century **textile mill** (9), now used for a display of antiques. Return up High Street.

At the top is a fine view of the Market Cross grouping well with the abbey behind it.

Marlborough

History. The castle mound, now in the grounds of the College, is thought to be prehistoric. The castle dated from the eleventh century. William the Conqueror had a mint there. Many royal events took place until the fifteenth century. The Seymour family built a house in the bailey close in 1621, and in the eighteenth century what was the Castle inn, and is now C House, Marlborough College, was built on the site. In the Civil War the

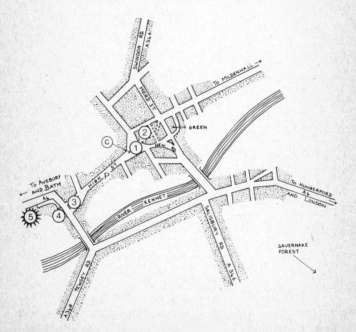

MARLBOROUGH

1. Town Hall
2. St Mary's church
3. Church of SS Peter and Paul
4. C House, Marlborough College
5. Castle mound

castle was for the King and the town for Parliament. The town was several times largely destroyed by fire, and no thatched buildings were allowed after 1690. The College was founded in 1843.

Approach by the main London-Bath road (A4), with the beautiful Savernake Forest on the left. Cross the river Kennet and enter High Street by New Road and past the Town Hall. High Street is remarkably wide (plate 17), and parking is allowed along the middle.

Walk. Start at the east end of High Street. Behind the **Town Hall** (1903) (1) is **St Mary's church** (2), with Classical seventeenth-century arcade, rebuilt after the fire of 1690. The tower is sixteenth-century. Beyond the church is The Green, with many charming houses. Return to High Street and note the colonnaded shops on the north side, and interesting houses of various dates on both sides. There are older buildings at the back of the north-side houses. At the west end is the **church of SS Peter and Paul**, partly fifteenth-century but restored, with prominent pinnacled tower (3). Beyond this is the **College**, including the very handsome **C House** (4) (see above) and the **castle mound** (5).

In the neighbourhood. Two and a half miles east, **Mildenhall** (pronounced 'Mynall') church has fascinating Georgian fittings.

Half a mile west of Marlborough **Preshute** church has a magnificent Tournai-marble font.

About five miles west of Marlborough, off the Bath road, is **Avebury**, with its wonderful stone circles and avenues, the mysterious **Silbury Hill**, and the West Kennet long barrow, as well as an interesting part-Saxon church, Elizabethan manor-house and museum.

The small town of **Pewsey**, seven miles south of Marlborough, gives its name to the beautiful Vale of Pewsey. It has a large church with Transitional Norman nave and much Victorian painting. A statue of King Alfred, in the middle of the town, was erected to celebrate the coronation of George V.

Melksham

History. Melksham was a royal manor in Saxon times, and was mentioned in Domesday Book. Edward I hunted from there in Chippenham Forest. Later the surrounding land was converted to agriculture and Melksham became a market town, and later again a cloth centre. In the nineteenth century a spa was started, with a pump room and handsome crescent of houses, but it could not compete with Bath and soon failed. John Fowler, inventor of

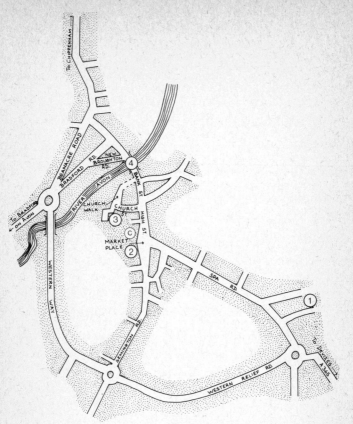

MELKSHAM

1. Spa
2. Town Hall
3. Church of St Michael and All Angels
4. Bridge

the first steam plough, was born in Melksham. The town is now the centre for rubber and other industries.

Approach by A365 from Devizes and turn into Spa Road at the first roundabout on the Western Relief Road. What remains of the **spa** can be seen down a small road on the right (1). Spa Road leads into the Market Place, and there is a car park by the **Town Hall** (1847) (2).

Walk. Turn north along High Street and left into Church Street, where there are some pleasant eighteenth-century houses. The **church**, St Michael and All Angels (3), is mainly Perpendicular, with a few traces of a former Norman one on the same site. It has some early Decorated nave arcades. From the church, proceed along Church Walk into Bank Street. Here is the eighteenth-century **bridge** (4) across the Bristol Avon, with handsome balustrades.

Salisbury

History. Old Sarum, from which Salisbury is descended, was originally an Iron Age camp, defended by large earthworks. It was used by the Romans, the Saxons and the Normans, all of whom improved the defences. The Normans built a castle and also established a bishopric and built a fine cathedral. This was finished by Bishop Osmund, Chancellor of England, in 1092. It was damaged in a storm, and rebuilt and enlarged by the next Bishop, Roger. He had a dispute with King Stephen, who seized the castle. Strife between castle and cathedral continued for about sixty years. In 1220 Bishop Poore, deciding that the site of Old Sarum was inconvenient, laid the foundations of a new cathedral two miles south of Old Sarum and built the city of Salisbury. The cathedral was entirely in the Early English style; the beautiful tower and famous spire (404 feet) were added in the next century. A detached bell-tower was very wrongly destroyed in the eighteenth century.

The city's first charter was granted by Henry III in 1227 and others were granted later, extending the city's rights and privileges. Salisbury has always been a flourishing market town, and in medieval times had many craft guilds. Many kings and queens have visited the city. The Duke of Buckingham was executed there in 1484 for rebelling against Richard III. Some fighting took place there during the Civil War. Charles II stayed in Salisbury to escape from the plague in London, and James II assembled an army there to oppose William of Orange, but without success; William himself was there very soon afterwards. The city is a centre of education, including the Theological College, the Diocesan Training College for Teachers, and many schools.

Approach. Enter Salisbury by London Road (A30), and shortly after crossing the railway, turn right at a large roundabout into Churchill Way. At the bottom of this turn left at another roundabout into Castle Street, from which a turning on the right leads into the main car park.

Walk 1. From the car park, go back into Castle Street and on down it into the Market Place (markets Tuesdays and Saturdays). A plaque by the entrance door of **Debenhams** (1) in Blue Boar Row, the north side of the Market Place, commemorates the Duke of Buckingham's execution (see above). South-west of the Market Place is **St Thomas's church** (2). It has a noteworthy 'Doom' wall-painting, showing some fine architecture of The Heavenly City, above the chancel arch, and some interesting monuments. The fifteenth-century **Poultry Cross** (3) stands at the junction of Silver Street and Minster Street, and opposite stand the **Haunch of Venison** (fifteenth to sixteenth centuries) (4) and other timber-framed houses. In **Butcher Row**, the south side of the Market Place, are gabled medieval houses. An alley leads into New Canal, so called from open streams which formerly ran through the streets. The **Halle of John Halle** (1470-83), a wool-merchant, has a noble roof. The street front was restored by Pugin, the nineteenth-century Gothic-revival architect, and is now the entrance to the Odeon cinema (5). A new arcade called Old George Mall leads from New Canal into High Street, and at the far end of it is the **Old George** inn (6), supported on its original timber framework. Shakespeare, Cromwell and Pepys were among its visitors. The last had 'a silk bed and a very good diet', but was 'mad' at the prices. On the corner of High Street and New Street is **Mitre House** (7), where bishops still robe for their enthronement. It is a tall, medieval building with a mitre painted on it; Bishop Poore's dwelling stood on this site. Opposite, on the corner of High Street and Crane Street, is the fourteenth-century timber-framed house, now **Beach's Bookshop** (8). Near this is the rich Perpendicular gateway of the Close (9). It has a royal arms on the north side and a statue of Edward VII on the south. On the left beyond this is the **Matrons' College** (1682) (10), probably designed by Wren, a friend of the founder, Bishop Seth Ward. It is for clergy widows. Opposite it is The Green. On the right of this is the magnificent **Mompesson House** (National Trust) (11), designed for Charles Mompesson, probably also by Wren when he was surveying the cathedral, c. 1701. Inside it has a richly carved staircase, and very good plaster decoration (open May to September, Wednesdays and Saturdays 2.30 p.m. to 6 p.m.; at other times by appointment).

The view of **Salisbury Cathedral** (plate 22), with its beautiful lawns, and lovely houses round the Close, is world-famous. The exterior of the cathedral is austerely beautiful; the west front, however, is richly ornamented, and takes the form of a huge screen with statues. The tower and spire are also much decorated. The interior is sometimes considered rather cold-looking, with its shafts of polished black marble against the grey Purbeck-marble columns which support the nave arcade. The old stained glass, which would have had a warming effect, was unfortunately removed, with many other beautiful features, by James Wyatt, the eighteenth-century 'restorer' who also had the detached campanile destroyed. Of the many remarkable tombs in the cathedral, he demolished some and moved others into different places; they are now mainly in two long lines on either side of the nave. Many are medieval, some later, and there are others in the transepts and choir. The entry to the eastern transepts is under inverted arches similar to those in Wells Cathedral. At the end of the north aisle is preserved the mechanism of a fourteenth-century clock, still working, now known to be the earliest of its kind in England.

The late thirteenth-century cloisters, approached from the south-west corner of the south transept, have beautiful windows in the geometrical Decorated style, with some fragments of old glass. The chapter house of the same period, with ribbed vaulting springing from a single column in the middle, is a beautiful, light building, and has a fascinating series of sculptures of the Old Testament.

Above the east walk of the cloisters is the cathedral library, full of historical documents, including one of the four surviving copies of Magna Carta. (More detailed descriptions of this glorious cathedral may be obtained in the building.)

Returning to the North Walk of the Close leads to **St Ann's Gate** (12). **Malmesbury House** (13), adjoining the gate on the left, was formerly the home of the Earl of Malmesbury. It is open from April to September on Wednesdays and Thursdays from 2 p.m. to 5 p.m., and contains excellent plasterwork and a fine eighteenth-century staircase. From it Lord Coventry, a supporter of Charles II, signalled across St John Street to other supporters at the **King's Arms** inn (14) while Charles was in hiding at Heale House. St Ann's Street, opposite the gate, has very interesting old houses, and off it to the right is a little street called **The Friary**, after a friary of the Franciscan order established in 1224; a few old buildings once formed part of it.

The very interesting **Salisbury and South Wiltshire Museum** (15) contains, among many other exhibits, prehistoric and other antiquities, a wonderful model of Old Sarum in its heyday, the figure of a giant formerly taken round the city in a midsummer procession of the Tailors' Guild, the hobby-horse on which the giant's page Hobnob rode, and a fine collection of porcelain. Cross the road into Dolphin Street and turn left into Barnard Street. **Trinity Hospital** (16) on the corner of Trinity Street dates from 1702 and has a one-handed clock in the turret; it was founded before 1379. **Ivy Street** is named after a mayor who, alone among

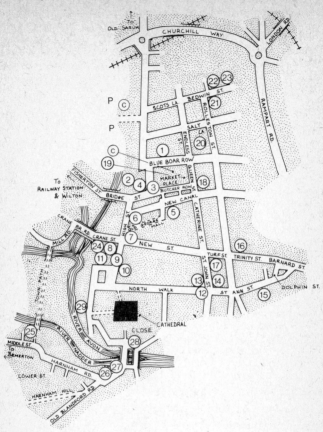

SALISBURY

1. Execution plaque
2. St Thomas's church
3. Poultry Cross
4. Haunch of Venison
5. Halle of John Halle
6. Old George inn
7. Mitre House
8. Beach's Bookshop
9. Close gateway
10. Matrons' College

11. Mompesson House
12. St Ann's Gate
13. Malmesbury House
14. King's Arms
15. Salisbury and South Wiltshire Museum
16. Trinity Hospital
17. White Hart
18. John a Port's House
19. Guildhall

20. Shoemakers' Guildhall
21. Frowde's Almshouses
22. St Edmund's church
23. Council House
24. Church House
25. Harnham Mill
26. All Saints' church
27. Rose and Crown
28. St Nicholas Hospital
29. King's House

the city authorities, stuck bravely to his post during the plague of 1627. On the corner of Ivy Street and St John Street is the old **White Hart** coaching inn (17). St John Street leads north into Catherine Street and this into Queen Street. On the right here is the 1425 **house of John a Port** (18), a wool-merchant, six times mayor. It is now a china shop, but visitors are welcome. Further on, on the left, is the **Guildhall** (19), designed in the eighteenth century by William Chambers and containing a good collection of portraits. Queen Street is the east side of the Market Place. Continue into **Endless Street** (a corruption of Endle's Street) and turn right into Salt Lane. Adjoining the Pheasant inn is the **Shoemakers' Guildhall** (20), left to the guild by Philip Crewe in 1638. Turn left into Rolleston Street and right into Bedwin Street. **Frowde's Almshouses** (21), on the corner, are of good eighteenth-century brickwork. **St Edmund's church** (22) is a completely Perpendicular building with a tower rebuilt in very late Gothic style in 1653, after the fall of its predecessor. The **Council House** (23), a fine sixteenth-century mansion, was once the house of the Wyndham family. In the grounds are earthworks, all that remains of the city ramparts, and the fifteenth-century north porch of the cathedral, moved there by Wyatt.

Return to the car park by Bedwin Street and Scot's Lane.

Walk 2 could start from Crane Street, where there is another car park. **Church House** (24) in Crane Street, formerly a wool-merchant's house, retains its good hall and arched gateway. Crane Street leads into Crane Bridge Road, which crosses two branches of the Avon. From Mill Road, Long Bridge crosses the Nadder and leads on to **Town Path**, from which is the wonderful view of the cathedral immortalised by Constable. The path leads to **Harnham Mill** (25) with a ground-floor of stone and flint chequer-work, and a fine open timbered roof inside. From here one can turn right along Middle Street and follow the very pretty riverside path to **Bemerton church**, of which George Herbert, the seventeenth-century poet, was vicar. Otherwise turn left down Lower Street and Harnham Road to **All Saints church** (26) and right into Old Blandford Road. A footpath on the right leads to **Harnham Hill**, from which there is a fine view of the city. Return to the church, pass the old **Rose and Crown** inn (27), and cross the Avon by the bridge built in 1245 by Bishop Bingham. On an island in the middle is a cottage, formerly a chapel. Beyond the bridge on the right is **St Nicholas Hospital** (28), also built by Bishop Bingham, for eight Sisters and four Brothers, who were to nurse the sick. Turn left into De Vaux Place, and into the Close by Harnham Gate. The **King's House** (29) with thirteenth-century porch, is now part of the Diocesan Training College. It takes its name from

James I who lodged there when in Salisbury. Richard III had also stayed there at the time of Buckingham's rebellion.

Leave the Close by the North Gate and turn left back into Crane Street by Beach's Bookshop.

In the neighbourhood. Old Sarum (see above) is easily reached by car along Castle Street and Castle Road, or by bus. It is a conical mound in three terraces. Much can be seen of the old fortifications, and the Norman appearance can be imagined after seeing the model in the Salisbury Museum.

Stonehenge is ten miles north, and can be reached by a pretty road through Stratford-sub-Castle and up the Avon valley.

Swindon

History. There were probably hill-top Saxon settlements, and certainly Norman ones, in old Swindon, and it was a market town of importance in medieval times. In Tudor times the Goddard family acquired much of the land, and in 1626 one of the Goddards obtained a charter from Charles I for a market and fair, and the little town became a prosperous centre of trade and agriculture.

The railway town, at the foot of the hill, started in 1835 when the Great Western Railway came to Swindon, and the famous locomotive works were opened in 1842. The town then grew rapidly until it became the largest in Wiltshire. Since 1950 there has been a huge development of industry, housing, technical college, traffic-free shopping precincts and the like, so that the town presents most interesting contrasts.

Approach. Richard Jeffries, the Wiltshire naturalist, lived in Swindon. His house, now a museum (1), is on the left as one approaches Swindon from Marlborough, about two miles short of the town centre, just after Day House Lane and near Coate water reservoir, now an open space for leisure and sport. Where Marlborough Road leads into High Street, there is a car park on the right.

Walk 1. In the Market Square is the old **Town Hall** (2), (now business premises) in the Grecian style with an Italianate tower. On the right of High Street is the **Goddard Arms**, a charming, long, low brick building (3). High Street leads into **Cricklade Street**, where No. 42, on the right, is considered one of the best town houses in Wiltshire (4). Dating from 1729, it is of brick with stone dressings and many notable features. A little further on, also on the right, is **Christ Church** (5), a very good Gothic Revival building by Sir Gilbert Scott (1851). Turn back, and right into Wood Street, and on into Bath Street. Immediately on the right is the **Museum and Art Gallery** (c. 1830) (6), with Doric front. It includes old pictures of Swindon and natural history exhibits.

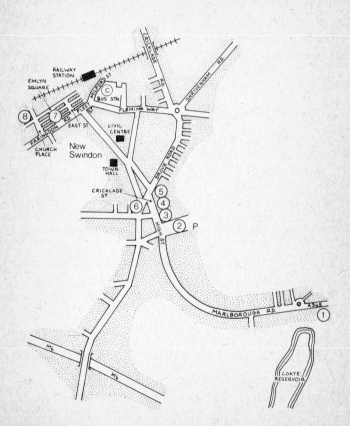

SWINDON

1. Richard Jeffries's house
2. Old Town Hall
3. Goddard Arms
4. No. 42 Cricklade Street
5. Christ Church
6. Museum and Art Gallery
7. Railway Museum
8. St Mark's church

Walk 2. Modern Swindon lies below this, but the best way to reach the railway town is to return to the car, drive down High Street, Cricklade Street and Drove Road, and at the roundabout at the bottom turn left into Fleming Way, and on into Fleet Street and Faringdon Road, in which is the **Railway Museum** (7) (plate 20), containing several famous locomotives. The stone cottages between East Street and Church Place (c. 1840) were built for the railway workers and, with **St Mark's Church** (8) (Gilbert Scott) and the **Mechanics' Institute** in Emlyn Square, form one of the earliest examples of a planned housing estate.

In the neighbourhood. Lydiard Tregoze, about three miles west of Swindon, was bought by the Corporation in 1943. There is a fine mansion (now a conference centre), formerly home of the Bolingbrokes, rebuilt in the Classical style by John, Viscount St John, c. 1745; it has some remarkable plaster ceilings. It is open to the public, Wednesdays to Saturdays inclusive, and bank holidays except Boxing Day, 10.30 a.m. to 12.30 p.m. and 2 p.m. to 5.30 p.m., October to March, and 10.30 a.m. to 12.30 p.m. and 2 p.m. to 8 p.m., April to September.

The **church** nearby has some twelfth-century work, but is mainly rather later. It has a wonderful collection of monuments, including 'The Golden Cavalier', Edward St John, killed in the Civil War in 1645. Other noteworthy features are the chancel screen with royal arms of James I on both sides, the sanctuary rails and gates of excellent seventeenth-century metalwork, and the painted chancel roof.

Trowbridge

History. Trowbridge is the administrative centre of Wiltshire, although Salisbury still ranks as the county town. There was probably a Saxon settlement on the river Biss. A Norman castle was built by Humphrey de Bohun, and was held for Empress Matilda in her conflict with King Stephen. Trowbridge became a royal manor under Henry IV.

From early times until today, Trowbridge has been one of the centres of the West of England cloth industry. It is a fine town, with many beautiful houses dating from the time of the cloth trade's greatest prosperity.

Approach either from Devizes by A361, or from Westbury by A363, carefully following signs to the town centre. From the Town Hall in Market Street turn left into Castle Street, off which car parks will be found (situations changing at time of writing).

Walk. From the **Town Hall** (1) walk down Fore Street. Some of the best houses are the **Midland Bank** (2), **Lloyds Bank** (3), and an impressive group in the part of Fore Street called **The Parade** (4). Fore Street leads to Wicker Hill, with the **Town Bridge** (c. 1777) (5) at the bottom, with a stone **lock-up** (1758) beside it. Return to Fore Street, and turn off into Castle Street and Court Street, where some of the cloth-mills stand. Returning to the Town Hall, walk eastward along Silver Street and Roundstone Street, where there are many more fine houses of various dates. Now turn up Church Street and left into Church Walk. The **parish church of St James**

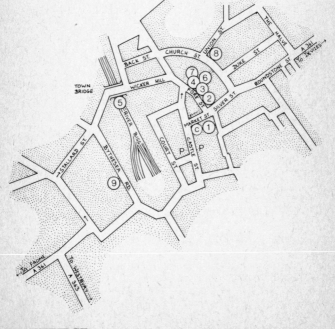

TROWBRIDGE

1. Town Hall
2. Midland Bank
3. Lloyds Bank
4. The Parade
5. Town Bridge
6. Parish church of St James
7. Rectory
8. Almshouses
9. County Hall

(6) was built on the site of an earlier one by James Terumber, a wealthy clothier, c. 1483. It is mainly Perpendicular, and has a graceful stone spire, 160 feet high. Three Norman tombstones are preserved at the west end of the church, one inscribed in Latin to 'our child Adelina'. The **Rectory** (7), north-west of the church, is a charming gabled house. George Crabbe, the poet, was rector there from 1814 to 1872, when he died. His monument is in the church. In the churchyard is a tomb (plate 21) erected by cloth-workers to Thomas Helliker, executed in the early nineteenth-century for refusing to betray the ringleader of the anti-machinery riots. **Almshouses** (8) at the corner of Union Street, c. 1861, have stone arcaded ground floor, and upper floor of timbered balconies with gables.

The **County Hall** (9), a good neo-Georgian building (1938-40), is in the rather curiously-named Bythesea Road.

Warminster

History. Warminster has a very early history. Bronze Age people inhabited **Cop Heap** (1), a wooded hill within the modern boundaries of the town. The town itself dates from Saxon times. King Alfred stayed there, and it was a royal manor until the time of Henry II.

In the Middle Ages it was an important centre of the cloth industry, and later both Defoe and Cobbett referred to it as one of the greatest corn markets in England. It now has many other industries and is also a military centre.

Approach from Salisbury by A36 and drive straight along Boreham Road, East Street, Market Place, High Street and George Street, turn left into Samborne Road and left again into the Western car park.

Walk. Across Samborne Road is Emwell Street. The **Weymouth Arms** (2) on the left has a grand pedimented porch and, inside, good panelling and an old stone fireplace. Emwell Street leads into Vicarage Street, with **Wren House** (3) on the right. Turn back and left into Church Street. On the left is an **obelisk** (4) and on the right a very handsome building, formerly St Boniface College, now part of **Lord Weymouth's Grammar School** (5). Arnold of Rugby was at school there as a young boy. The **Minster Church of St Denys** (6) is largely Perpendicular, considerably restored. It has a Norman arch in the north transept. The organ, dating from 1792, was presented to Salisbury Cathedral by George III, but was not powerful enough, and was sold to the citizens of Warminster.

Turn back down Church Street, left along Silver Street and George Street, and fork left into Portway. **Portway House** (7), on the left, now council offices, is a fine Georgian house, with beautiful wrought iron gates well restored in 1965. Return down Portway and left into High Street, where there are many good Georgian buildings, including the **Bath Arms hotel** (8), and the **Old Bell** (9), founded originally in the fourteenth century, with its colonnaded front. **St Laurence Chapel** (10), founded in Edward I's time, has been largely rebuilt, but retains its early Perpendicular tower. It was bought by the citizens in 1575 for £36 6s 8d. The **Town Hall** (11) was built in Jacobean style by Sir Edward Blore in 1830, and presented to the town by the Marquess of Bath in 1903. A footpath leads from High Street into the Western car park.

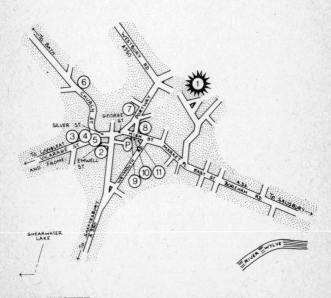

WARMINSTER

1. Cop Heap
2. Weymouth Arms
3. Wren House
4. Obelisk
5. Lord Weymouth's Grammar School
6. Minster Church of St Denys
7. Portway House
8. Bath Arms
9. Old Bell
10. St Laurence Chapel
11. Town Hall

In the neighbourhood. Two miles west, along the A362 Frome road, is the famous **Longleat House** and park, seat of the Marquess of Bath (open daily except Christmas). On the right of A362 here is **Cley Hill** (National Trust (800 feet), an outlier of the chalk downs, topped by an Iron Age camp. South-west is the beautiful **Shearwater Lake:** leave Warminster by the Weymouth and Shaftesbury road and turn right at Longbridge Deverill.

Westbury

History. Westbury, on the western edge of Salisbury Plain, was probably inhabited in very early times. Relics of Romano-British domestic arts have been found there and are in Devizes Museum. Domesday Book shows that William the Conqueror owned

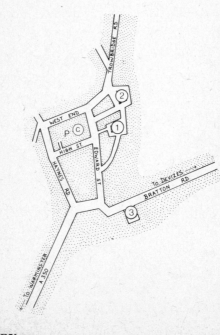

WESTBURY

1. All Saints' church
2. Town Hall

3. Prospect Square

Westbury Manor. Many noteworthy people have lived there, and Sir Robert Peel once represented Westbury in Parliament. Cloth was once the main industry; now, owing to Westbury's good position as a road and railway centre, it has other industries, including cement.

Approach from Warminster by A350, turn left into Haynes Road and right into High Street. The car park is on the left.

Walk. At the other end of High Street, turn right into Edward Street and left into Church Street, where there are some attractive old houses. The **church**, All Saints (1), is Perpendicular, with central tower. It has some good monuments, and the Mauduit Chapel on the north side of the chancel and Willoughby de Broke Chapel on the south. There is a chained copy of the New Testament paraphrase by Erasmus who used to stay in the neighbourhood. North of the church is the Market Place, in which are the old **Town Hall** (2) and some good Georgian houses. Return to Edward Street and left at the end of it into Bratton Road. On the right is **Prospect Square** (3), an interesting example of working-class housing, laid out by a cloth manufacturer, Abraham Laverton, in 1870.

The **Westbury White Horse**, at Bratton, is thought to date from 1700, but was recut in 1778.

Wilton

History. Wilton is one of the oldest boroughs in England. Indeed, it was from Egbert's 'Royal Borough of Wilton', in 838, that he proclaimed the union of Wessex and Kent, and so made himself first king of England. Even before that, in 770, Wilton had had a religious house. This became in turn a Benedictine priory and an abbey, and the Abbess of Wilton held very high precedence. Edith, sister of Edward the Martyr, was brought up in the abbey, and built a church in Wilton c. 978. Many other princesses and queens were connected with the abbey, but unfortunately the Empress Matilda used it as a headquarters in her fight against Stephen, and it was burnt down. Henry I granted the town a charter in 1100, and many other charters were granted, including one by Queen Victoria in 1885. These still exist, and may be seen on application to the town clerk. The town has been a centre of the sheep trade for centuries, and still has three sheep fairs every year. The carpet factory is also centuries old, the oldest building dating from 1655. The carpet weavers were granted a royal charter by William III in 1699.

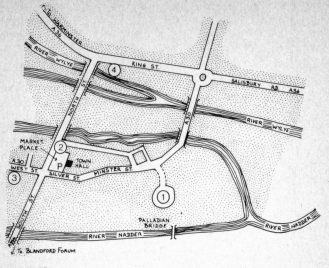

WILTON

1. Wilton House
2. St Mary's church
3. Church of SS Mary and Nicholas
4. Royal Carpet Factory

Wilton House, on the site of the abbey, has been the seat of the Earls of Pembroke since 1551, the abbey lands having been granted to William Herbert, the first earl.

Approach by A36 (the Warminster road) from Salisbury, turn left at the roundabout into A30, and **Wilton House** (1) is some way down on the left (free car park for visitors). The house is open from March to October, Tuesdays to Saturdays inclusive, and bank holidays from 11 a.m. to 6 p.m. (weekdays), 2 p.m. to 6 p.m. (Sundays). The last guided tour of the house is at 5.30 p.m. The outside of the house is by Wyatt and Inigo Jones, and there are fine state rooms by the latter, including the famous 'Double Cube'. There are beautiful portraits by Van Dyck and other famous painters, and other works of art and historical interest. In the park are giant cedars of Lebanon, some dating from 1630, and a Palladian bridge across the Nadder, by Roger Morris (1737).

After leaving Wilton House, drive on along A30, Minster Street and Silver Street, to the car park in the Market Place on the right.

Walk. The old parish church, **St Mary's** (2), with a ruined nave and only the chancel intact, is in the north-west corner of the Market Place. The present parish church **SS Mary and Nicholas** (3), a remarkable Lombardic-style building, with tall campanile and rich interior, is in West Street. In this street there are also several charming old houses. The **Royal Carpet Factory** (4), King Street, may be visited by appointment.

Wootton Bassett

History. Wootton Bassett, a pretty little hill-top town between Marlborough and Cricklade, was given its first charter by Henry VI, and this was renewed by Elizabeth I and Charles II. The town

WOOTTON BASSETT

1. Town Hall
2. All Saints' church

3. Angel hotel
4. Cross Keys inn

returned two members to Parliament from the fifteenth century until the Reform Act of 1832.

Approach. Coming from Marlborough by the beautiful downland road, B4041, turn right into High Street. This is very wide and car parking is allowed along the sides of the streets.

Walk. The **Town Hall** (1), half-timbered and supported on stone pillars, stands in the middle of the street towards the south-west end. It was built by Laurence Hyde, Lord Rochester, in 1700, and restored by Lady Meux in 1907. The **church** (2), All Saints, is just beyond the Town Hall. Originally thirteenth-century, it was largely restored by Street in 1870. The nave has an old panelled roof, and there is a vaulted south porch with parvise. There are some good houses, some of stone and some of brick, in High Street. They are mainly early Georgian, and include the **Angel** hotel (3), the **Cross Keys** inn (4) and several others worth notice.

Index

141

INDEX

Printed by C. I. Thomas & Sons (Haverfordwest) Ltd., Press Buildings,
Merlin's Bridge, Haverfordwest, Pembrokeshire.